i

The Tyranny of Belief

How Religion Suppresses
Free Thought

Ethan Knight

Distinct Press Publishing.
www.DistinctPress.com

The views expressed in this work are the author's own and may not
reflect the opinions or policies of any organization or individual.
Readers are encouraged to form their own conclusions based on the
content presented. The author assumes no responsibility for the
reader's actions. References to people, organizations, or events are
based on the author's translation, recollection and/or interpretation.
This work does not provide professional advice and readers should
consult experts in relevant fields for guidance.

Library of Congress Cataloging-in-Publication Data

Knight, Ethan 1986-
        Tyranny of Belief: How Religion Suppresses Free
Thought. / Ethan Knight

Summary: "The Tyranny of Belief: How Religion Suppresses Free
Thought" by Ethan Knight examines the power dynamics and negative
consequences of religious belief systems. The book delves into
inconsistencies and contradictions in religious texts, exploring how
religion has been used as a tool to gain power, control, and influence
throughout history. It discusses various historical events such as the
Crusades, inquisition, witch hunts, colonization, and religious
conflicts that have perpetuated social inequalities and suppressed
dissent. The author also challenges religious beliefs and explores
alternative belief systems such as secular humanism, existentialism,
stoicism, humanism, rationalism, and skepticism. The book delves
into the absurdities of religious belief, hidden texts and mysteries, and
tensions within religion itself. – Provided by publisher.

ISBN 13: 978-1-943103-32-4

1. Religion & Spirituality > Religious Studies> Religious Intolerance
& Persecutionm2. Religion & Spirituality > Religious Studies>
History of Religions 3. Religion & Spirituality > Other Religions,
Practices & Sacred Texts > Religious Cults

Table of Contents

Introduction... xiii

Chapter One: The Power Play of Religion 17

Inconsistencies in Religious Texts.................. 19

Contradictions in Religious Texts.................... 30

Religion to Gain Power and Control...............39

The Crusades..39

The Inquisition......................................40

The Spanish Inquisition 41

Witch Hunts 41

The Salem Witch Trials 41

Colonization and Conversion of Native
Americans 42

Apartheid in South Africa...........................42

Forced Conversion of Indigenous Australians
....43

The Partition of India.................................43

Anti-Semitism..44

Religious Extremism...................................44

ISIS 44

Political Influence 45

Gender and Sexuality 45

Homophobia...................................46

Exploitation...................................46

Suppression of Dissent...................46

Indoctrination 47

Perpetuation of Social Inequalities 47

Televangelists 47

The Caste System in India 48

The Treatment of Women..............48

Religious Conflicts.........................49

Religious Persecution.....................49

Religious Nationalism....................49

Alternative Belief Systems 50

Secular Humanism 50

Existentialism................................52

Stoicism...53

Humanism 54

Rationalism 56

Skepticism 57

What Is Religion? 58

Absurdities of Religious Belief 62

The Six Days of Creation 62

Slavery, Genocide and Violence 64

The All-Knowing and Powerful 65

Sacrifices of Flesh and Blood 67

The Promise of an Afterlife 69

The Power of Prayer 71

The Divine Plan: Suffering and Tragedy 72

Eternal Damnation and Punishment 73

The Conspiracy of Science 75

Nobody's Perfect 76

Chapter Two: Tensions and Disputes within
Religion 79

Critics of Religion 79

Theological vs. Natural Morality 90

Theological Legends and Myths 92

Religious Imposters and God's Children 93

The Foundation of Reasoning 98

Atheists and Enemies 101

Anthropomorphizing Gods 102

Burned and Banned....................................105

The Council of Carthage 114

Chapter Three: Hidden Texts and Mysteries 117

Challenging The Christian Church 117

The Cathars 119

The Waldensians..121

The Hussites..122

The Lollards 123

The Protestant Reformation 125

Liberal Theology.......................................126

Liberation Theology..................................128

The Apocrypha...130

Mary Magdalene and Thomas...................154

Miracles 159

Jesus' Miracles...161

Parting of the Red Sea 164

The Ten Plagues of Egypt..........................165

The Walls of Jericho 166

The Story of Devil's and Swine.................167

Daniel In the Lion's Den............................168

The Devil and the Church..........................176

Fear and Superstition 178

The Pursuit of Truth...................................181

Jesus Christ 185

God's Decrees of the Order of Nature 187

Chapter Four: The Retelling 191

The Torah...191

Noah's Ark...192

One God...194

The Story of Creation 196

Adam and Eve..197

Crossing the Red Sea 200

The Story of Joseph 201

The Miracle of Manna................................202

The Brazen Serpent................................203

Pillars of Smoke and Fire............................204

Sacrificing the Daughter 206

Samson and the Lion................................207

Hyperbole................................209

The Tower of Babel 209

The Talking Serpent................................210

Flutes and Trumpets................................212

The Hermaphrodite 213

Resurrection and Immortality 214

Natural Phenomena................................215

The Garden of Eden 216

Christianity or Pagan Myths 218

Jesus' Conception 218

Water Into Wine................................219

To Hell and Back 220

More Miracles...221

The Infinite God..222

Chapter Five...225

Indigenous...227

Dr. Micheál Ledwith....................................229

Introduction

Religion has been a significant force in human society for thousands of years. It has provided individuals with a sense of community, meaning, and purpose, and has served as a guiding framework for morality and ethics. However, when religion is used as a means of control and domination, it can become a powerful tool of oppression, suppressing free thought and critical inquiry. The concept of the "tyranny of belief" refers to the ways in which religious beliefs and institutions can limit individual autonomy and stifle intellectual curiosity.

This book explores the history and contemporary manifestations of religious tyranny and its impact on free thought. The term "tyranny of belief" encompasses a range of practices and beliefs that restrict the free flow of ideas and limit individual expression. In many cases, these practices are enforced by religious institutions and authorities who seek to maintain power and control over their followers.

Throughout history, religion has been used as a means of suppressing free thought and dissent. Examples of this include the Inquisition, witch hunts, and the forced conversion of indigenous peoples. These practices have often been justified using religious doctrines and beliefs, such as the idea that those who do not conform to the dominant religious worldview are morally corrupt or even possessed by demons.

Today, religious tyranny continues to manifest itself in various forms. Religious cults, fundamentalist groups, and extremist organizations use their beliefs to justify acts of violence and discrimination. Religious dogma can limit individual autonomy and hinder scientific advancement, leading to a society that is resistant to change and new ideas.

The psychological and societal impacts of religious tyranny are far-reaching. People who are subject to religious oppression may experience cognitive dissonance, self-censorship, and a loss of personal autonomy. Additionally, religious tyranny can hinder social progress and scientific advancement, contributing to a society that is less open-minded and less willing to question authority.

Despite the negative effects of religious tyranny, there are alternative approaches to spirituality and morality that do not rely on religious beliefs. Secular humanism, for example, emphasizes critical thinking and personal autonomy, offering a path towards greater intellectual freedom and personal growth.

This book aims to highlight the ways in which religion can be used as a tool of oppression and the importance of promoting free thought and critical inquiry in today's society.

Chapter One: The Power Play of Religion

The origins of religion are difficult to trace because they predate written history. However, it is believed that religion emerged as a way for early humans to understand and explain natural phenomena, such as thunderstorms, earthquakes, and the changing seasons. They believed that these phenomena were caused by supernatural forces and that appeasing these forces through ritual and sacrifice would ensure their survival and prosperity.

As human societies became more complex, so too did their religious beliefs and practices. Religious figures such as priests, shamans, and prophets emerged, who were believed to have special access to the supernatural realm and the ability to communicate with the gods.

Throughout history, religion has played a central role in shaping culture, politics, and society. It has been used to justify political power, as well as to promote social cohesion and morality. Religion has also been a source of conflict and violence, with wars and persecution often being carried out in the name of religious beliefs.

Over time, religions have evolved and adapted to changing cultural, social, and political circumstances. New religious movements have emerged, while others have declined or disappeared altogether. The development of science and technology has also challenged many religious beliefs, leading to conflicts between science and religion.

Today, religion continues to be a significant force in many parts of the world, with billions of people identifying with various religious traditions. In this book, I would like people to recognize that religion has been a product of human culture and society, shaped by political, economic, and social factors.

In early human societies, religion played a significant role in explaining the natural world and providing a sense of community and order. Religious beliefs were closely tied to the daily lives of people, and religious rituals and ceremonies were often used to maintain social cohesion and order.

As human societies became more complex and stratified, religion became more institutionalized and organized. Priests, shamans, and other religious leaders emerged as intermediaries between people and the divine, and religious hierarchies developed. These hierarchies often reflected and reinforced existing social hierarchies, with religious leaders having significant power and influence over their followers.

Religion has also been used to legitimize political power and to control and manipulate the masses. Rulers throughout history have used religion to justify their rule and to maintain social control. Religious institutions have often been closely aligned with political power, and religious leaders have often played key roles in political decision-making.

In modern times, religion has continued to evolve and adapt to changing social and cultural contexts. Many religious traditions have experienced significant changes in their beliefs, practices, and institutions in response to new ideas, technologies, and social movements. The role of religion in society has also changed, with some religious institutions playing a more limited role in public life, while others continue to play a significant role in shaping social and political norms.

Inconsistencies in Religious Texts

The Holy Bible has been rewritten and edited numerous times throughout history. The *Old Testament* was originally written in Hebrew, while the New Testament was written in Greek. Over time, these texts were translated into various languages, including Latin, English, and others.

The process of editing and revising the biblical text has been ongoing for centuries, with different versions and translations emerging over time. For example, the *King James Version*, one of the most widely used English translations of the *Bible*, was first published in 1611 and has undergone numerous revisions and updates since then.

In addition, various councils and committees have been formed throughout history to determine which books should be included in the biblical canon and to standardize the text. The Council of Carthage in 397 AD, for instance, established the canon of the *New Testament* that is recognized by most Christian denominations today.

Certainly, this is one of the reasons there are several inconsistencies found in the various religious texts. I leave it to you to ponder some of these.

In the *Bible*, it is said that God created light before he created the sun and stars, which are the source of light. Where did this light come from and what was it?

The *Bible* states that God is all-loving and all-merciful, yet there are numerous examples of him ordering or committing acts of violence and genocide. Would an all-loving God call for this?

The *Bible* contains two different creation stories in the book of Genesis that differ in the order of creation and other details.

The first creation story in *Genesis 1:1-2:3* describes God creating the world in six days. On the first day, God creates light and separates it from darkness. On the second day, God creates the sky and separates the waters. On the third day, God creates dry land and vegetation. On the fourth day, God creates the sun, moon, and stars. On the fifth day, God creates sea creatures and birds. On the sixth day, God creates land animals and humans.

The second creation story in *Genesis 2:4-25* provides a different account of the creation of humans and the Garden of Eden. It describes God creating Adam from the dust of the ground and then creating Eve from one of Adam's ribs. In this story, God plants a garden in Eden and places Adam in it. God instructs Adam not to eat from the tree of the knowledge of good and evil, but Eve is later tempted by the serpent and eats from the tree, leading to their expulsion from the garden.

The first creation story in *Genesis* describes God creating the universe in six days, with each day representing a different aspect of creation, such as light, the sky, and living creatures. God creates humans last, male and female together, and gives them dominion over all the other living creatures.

The second creation story in *Genesis* describes God creating the first man, Adam, out of the dust of the ground and then creating a garden called Eden for him to live in. Later, God creates the first woman, Eve, out of one of Adam's ribs, and they live together in the garden. In this story, humans are created before the animals, and there is no mention of God creating the universe in a particular number of days.

So which one are we supposed to believe?

The *Bible* states that God is unchanging, yet his behavior and attitudes towards humanity appear to change throughout the course of the Old and New Testaments.

Here just a few examples of changes in God's behavior and attitudes towards humanity in the *Old and New Testaments*:

In the *Old Testament*, God is often portrayed as a vengeful and wrathful deity, punishing the Israelites for their disobedience and sending plagues and disasters upon them. However, in the *New Testament*, God is depicted as a merciful and forgiving figure, offering salvation to all who believe in Jesus Christ.

In the *Old Testament*, God commands the Israelites to engage in violent acts, such as killing the Canaanites and other neighboring tribes, as a means of securing their place in the promised land. In the *New Testament*, Jesus teaches a message of love and nonviolence, instructing his followers to turn the other cheek and love their enemies.

In the *Old Testament*, God establishes a covenant with the Israelites, promising to protect and bless them if they remain faithful to him. However, in the *New Testament*, God expands his salvation to include all people, not just the Israelites, through the sacrifice of Jesus Christ.

In the *Old Testament*, God is often depicted as having a very personal and direct relationship with his people, speaking to them through prophets and performing miracles to demonstrate his power. However, in the *New Testament*, God becomes more distant and mysterious, speaking through parables and leaving many questions unanswered.

In light of these inconsistencies, how then do religious believers reconcile these discrepancies and continue to maintain their faith in the infallibility and consistency of religious texts and beliefs?

Many religious texts contain accounts of miracles and supernatural events that are inconsistent with the laws of nature and science.

The parting of the Red Sea in the Hebrew *Bible* defies the laws of physics and the natural world because it suggests that Moses was able to manipulate water in a way that is impossible according to scientific principles. The *Bible* describes the sea as being divided into two walls of water, with the Israelites walking on dry land in the middle. This kind of separation of water would require a force that is not present in nature, such as a powerful wind or earthquake. It is also difficult to imagine how such an event could have taken place without leaving any geological evidence.

The virgin birth of Jesus in the Christian *Bible* defies the laws of biology and genetics because it suggests that Mary was able to conceive a child without the involvement of a human father. This is not possible according to current scientific knowledge, as reproduction in mammals requires the fusion of sperm and egg. The *Bible* attributes this miraculous conception to divine intervention, which is not something that can be explained or demonstrated by science.

The resurrection of Jesus from the dead in the Christian *Bible* defies the laws of biology and physics because it suggests that a dead body can come back to life. This is not possible according to scientific principles, which dictate that once biological functions have ceased, they cannot be restarted. The *Bible* attributes this event to divine intervention, but it is not something that can be verified or explained through empirical observation or experimentation.

The splitting of the moon in Islamic tradition defies the laws of physics and astronomy because it suggests that Muhammad was able to physically divide the moon into two separate parts. This is not possible according to scientific principles, as the moon is a large celestial body with a fixed structure and composition. It is also difficult to imagine how such an event could have taken place without leaving any observable effects on the moon's surface or orbit.

The *Bible* contains numerous contradictions and inconsistencies, such as different accounts of the genealogy of Jesus in the books of *Matthew* and *Luke*.

One such example is the genealogy of Jesus in the books of *Matthew* and *Luke*, which contain different names and lineages. In *Matthew*'s account, the genealogy traces Jesus' lineage through his adoptive father Joseph and back to Abraham. However, in *Luke*'s account, the genealogy traces Jesus' lineage through his mother Mary and back to Adam.

Another example of inconsistency within the *Bible* is the different accounts of the resurrection of Jesus. The four *Gospels* contain different details about the events leading up to and following the resurrection, such as the number and identity of the women who visited the tomb and the timing of when the resurrected Jesus appeared to his disciples.

There are also discrepancies in the accounts of Jesus' crucifixion. For example, the *Gospel of Mark* describes Jesus being crucified at the third hour, while the *Gospel of John* suggests that Jesus was not crucified until the sixth hour.

Another contradiction is found in the accounts of the Last Supper. The *Synoptic Gospels* (*Matthew, Mark*, and *Luke*) describe the Last Supper as a Passover meal, while the *Gospel of John* suggests that it occurred the day before Passover.

Additionally, there are discrepancies in the accounts of the birth and infancy of Jesus. The *Gospel of Matthew* suggests that Jesus was born during the reign of King Herod, while the *Gospel of Luke* places his birth during the time of a census under Quirinius. Furthermore, the *Gospel of Matthew* describes the family fleeing to Egypt to escape Herod's persecution, while the *Gospel of Luke* does not mention this.

The concept of an all-knowing, all-powerful God is at odds with the idea of human free will, since the actions of humans cannot be truly free if they are predetermined by God.

The idea of human free will suggests that individuals are able to make choices and decisions independently of external influences, including the influence of God.

However, the notion of an all-knowing, all-powerful God suggests that God is aware of all events that have occurred and will occur, and that God has the power to control or influence these events. This creates a paradox, since if God already knows what choices and decisions individuals will make, then these choices and decisions cannot truly be free.

For example, if God knows that an individual will choose to eat a particular type of food for lunch, then it could be argued that the individual's decision to do so is not truly a free choice. If God is all-powerful and can influence events, then it is possible that God could have caused the individual to make a different choice, which would also suggest that the individual's choice was not truly free.

Furthermore, if God has predetermined all events, then it raises questions about the role of human agency and responsibility. If all events are predetermined by God, then it could be argued that humans are not truly responsible for their actions, since their actions are determined by God's plan. This would raise questions about the morality of punishing individuals for their actions if they were not truly able to make free choices.

The concept of an afterlife or eternal punishment is often based on the belief that individuals will be judged according to certain criteria, such as adherence to a particular religious faith or moral code. However, the criteria used to determine who is granted eternal reward and who is punished are often arbitrary and subjective.

For example, in some religions, simply believing in a certain deity or set of religious doctrines is enough to ensure eternal reward, regardless of one's actions or moral character. This can be seen as arbitrary, as it implies that one's beliefs are more important than one's actions or character.

Similarly, the criteria used to determine who is deserving of eternal punishment can also be arbitrary. In some religions, simply failing to adhere to a certain set of moral codes or engaging in certain behaviors is enough to warrant eternal punishment, regardless of the context or circumstances surrounding those actions.

This can be problematic because it raises questions about justice and fairness. If eternal reward or punishment is based on arbitrary criteria, then it can be argued that the system is inherently unjust and unfair. It also creates a sense of fear and anxiety for individuals who may be uncertain about their eternal fate, leading to a potential suppression of critical thinking and exploration of alternative beliefs and perspectives.

Many religious texts contain sexist, racist, or

homophobic language or ideas that are no longer acceptable in modern society. Below are some examples of sexist, racist, or homophobic language or ideas found in religious texts:

Sexism: The *Bible* states in 1 *Timothy 2:11-12* that women should be silent and not have authority over men, and that they should learn in quietness and full submission. This passage has been used to justify the exclusion of women from leadership positions in many religious organizations.

Racism: *The Book of Mormon*, a sacred text in the Church of Jesus Christ of Latter-day Saints, contains numerous passages that suggest dark-skinned people are cursed and inferior to light-skinned people. This has been used to justify racist attitudes towards people of color.

Homophobia: *Leviticus 18:22* in the *Bible* states that homosexuality is an "abomination," and in *1 Corinthians 6:9-10*, it is listed alongside other sins such as adultery and theft. These passages have been used to justify discrimination and persecution against LGBTQ+ individuals.

Sexism: In the *Bhagavad Gita*, a Hindu text, it is stated that women are of a lower caste and are inferior to men. This has been used to justify gender inequality and discrimination against women in India and other parts of the world.

Homophobia: *The Hadith*, a collection of sayings attributed to the Prophet Muhammad in Islam, contains several passages that condemn homosexuality and call for the punishment of those who engage in homosexual acts. This has been used to justify discrimination and persecution against LGBTQ+ individuals in some Muslim-majority countries.

These examples illustrate how religious texts can contain language and ideas that are harmful and discriminatory towards certain groups of people. It is important to critically examine these texts and challenge such harmful beliefs and the hate and separation they cause.

Contradictions in Religious Texts

There are also numerous contradictions found in the various religious texts. Below are just a few to ponder.

In the *New Testament*, the *Gospel of Matthew*

and the *Gospel of Luke* both provide genealogies of Jesus, but they differ in significant ways. *Matthew*'s genealogy includes several more generations than *Luke*'s, and the names of some of the ancestors are different. Here are some of the differences:

Different Starting Points: *Matthew*'s genealogy starts with Abraham, the father of the Jewish people, while *Luke*'s genealogy traces Jesus' ancestry all the way back to Adam, the first man in the Bible.

Different Numbers of Generations: *Matthew*'s genealogy includes 42 generations from Abraham to Jesus, while *Luke*'s genealogy includes 77 generations.

Different Names: *Matthew*'s genealogy includes some different names than *Luke*'s genealogy, particularly in the later generations. For example, *Matthew*'s genealogy lists the father of Joseph as Jacob, while *Luke*'s genealogy lists his name as Heli. *Matthew* also includes several kings of Judah in his genealogy, while *Luke* does not.

Different Sequence: *Matthew*'s genealogy is arranged in a more structured and symmetrical way, with three sets of 14 generations each. *Luke*'s genealogy is less structured, and some of the names appear in a different order than in *Matthew*'s genealogy.

The *Bible* contains passages that advocate for both pacifism and violence. For example, Jesus teaches his followers to turn the other cheek, but in other parts of the *Old Testament*, God orders the Israelites to engage in warfare.

Regarding the contradiction between pacifism and violence in the *Bible*, one possible explanation is that these ideas reflect the different historical and cultural contexts in which they were written. For example, the pacifist teachings of Jesus may reflect the nonviolent resistance movements that were common in the first century CE, while the violent passages in the *Old Testament* may reflect the reality of warfare and conflict in ancient times.

But doesn't this then show us that the *Bible* and its teachings could have been interpreted or manipulated to fit the time?

Throughout history, individuals and groups have used religious texts like the *Bible* to amass people to their belief or agenda. This has often involved interpreting passages in a way that supports a particular political or social agenda, even if it goes against the original intent of the text.

One way this has been done is by using selective quoting or interpretation of passages to support a particular agenda. For example, in the United States, some religious groups have used passages from the *Bible* to support political positions on issues like abortion, homosexuality, and immigration. They may use quotes from the *Bible* out of context or emphasize certain passages while downplaying others to support their position.

Another way religious texts like the *Bible* have been used to amass people to a particular belief or agenda is through the creation of new interpretations or translations. This can involve changing the language or interpretation of certain passages to fit a particular ideology or agenda. For example, during the Protestant Reformation, Martin Luther created a German translation of the *Bible* that emphasized the importance of individual faith over religious hierarchy, which helped to support his ideas of reform.

Religious texts like the *Bible* have also been used to justify violence or oppression. For example, during the Crusades, Christians used passages from the *Bible* to justify their military campaigns against Muslims in the Holy Land. Similarly, during the era of slavery in the United States, some slave owners used the *Bible* to justify the practice, citing passages that they believed supported the idea that slavery was divinely ordained.

During the early Christian period, there were numerous different versions of the *Bible*, and different Christian sects often had their own preferred versions. In the fourth century CE, the Council of Nicaea was convened to standardize Christian doctrine and establish a canon of scripture. This resulted in the compilation of what is now known as the *New Testament*.

However, even after the canon was established, there were still debates and disagreements over the interpretation of biblical texts, leading to further changes and revisions. In the 16th century, for example, the Protestant Reformation resulted in new translations and interpretations of the *Bible*, as reformers sought to challenge the authority of the Catholic Church.

Moreover, translations of the *Bible* into different languages and cultural contexts have also resulted in changes and adaptations to the original texts. For example, early translations of the *Bible* into English, such as the *King James Version*, were influenced by the political and religious views of the time, and certain passages were changed or interpreted in ways that supported the prevailing ideologies.

In some cases, religious leaders or groups may also use their interpretation of religious texts to gain power or control over others. They may create strict interpretations of religious laws or rules that are used to regulate the behavior of their followers and punish those who do not comply. This can lead to a situation where people are afraid to challenge or question the religious authority, which can lead to abuses of power.

The process of rewriting and adapting the biblical texts to suit different purposes has been a complex and ongoing one throughout history, with different groups and individuals using the Bible to support their own beliefs, agendas, and power structures.

The contradiction regarding the date of Jesus' birth arises because the *Gospel of Matthew* and the *Gospel of Luke* provide different accounts of the historical events surrounding his birth. In *Matthew's Gospel*, the account describes the visit of the magi to King Herod, who becomes fearful that the newly born king would pose a threat to his rule. Herod orders the massacre of all male infants in Bethlehem under two years of age, which places Jesus' birth around 4 BCE, the year Herod is believed to have died.

In contrast, the *Gospel of Luke* places Jesus' birth during a census conducted by the Roman emperor Augustus, which led Mary and Joseph to travel to Bethlehem for the registration. The gospel also mentions the appearance of angels to shepherds who were watching their flocks at night, announcing the birth of a savior. Historically, the census mentioned in *Luke*'s gospel is believed to have taken place around 6 or 7 CE, which would place Jesus' birth several years after the death of King Herod.

The difference in the accounts of Judas Iscariot's death in the *Bible* is another prime example of how the different books of the *Bible* can present differing versions of the same event. In the *Gospel of Matthew*, it is written that Judas Iscariot, after betraying Jesus, felt remorse and returned the thirty pieces of silver he received from the priests who wanted to kill Jesus. He then went out and hanged himself.

However, in the *Book of Acts*, it is written that after betraying Jesus, Judas went out to a field, where he fell headfirst and his body burst open, spilling his intestines. The text goes on to explain that the field was called the "Field of Blood," named so because it was bought with the money that Judas received for betraying Jesus.

Elaborating on these contradictions, some biblical passages depict heaven as a physical place with streets of gold and gates made of pearls, while others describe it as a spiritual realm. For example, the *Book of Revelation* describes heaven as a city with walls and foundations, while the *Gospel of John* suggests that heaven is a state of being rather than a physical place.

Similarly, the concept of hell in the *Bible* is also contradictory. Some passages describe it as a place of eternal torment, with fire and brimstone, while others suggest that it is simply a place of separation from God. For example, the *Book of Revelation* describes hell as a place of eternal torment, while *the Gospel of Luke* suggests that it is a place of darkness and weeping and gnashing of teeth.

It seems the concepts of heaven and hell have evolved over time, with different religious traditions and denominations interpreting them in different ways. For example, the concept of purgatory in Catholicism is not found in the *Bible* but is instead a later development in Christian theology.

The *Bible* also contains numerous inconsistencies regarding the teachings of Jesus. In some passages, Jesus emphasizes the importance of helping the poor and marginalized, while in others he teaches that wealth and material possessions are blessings from God.

In some passages, Jesus stresses the importance of helping the poor and oppressed, such as when he declares that "Blessed are the poor in spirit, for theirs is the kingdom of heaven" (*Matthew 5:3*) and when he instructs his followers to sell their possessions and give to the poor (*Luke 12:33*). Jesus also criticizes the rich and warns of the dangers of greed and materialism, such as when he says, "It is easier for a camel to go through the eye of a needle than for a rich person to enter the kingdom of God" (*Mark 10:25*).

However, in other passages, Jesus appears to bless those who are wealthy and prosperous, such as when he tells the parable of the rich man and Lazarus (*Luke 16:19-31*), where the rich man is not condemned for his wealth but for his failure to help the poor. Additionally, Jesus often uses agricultural metaphors, such as the parable of the sower (*Matthew 13:1-23*), where the seed that falls on good soil produces a great harvest, indicating that material prosperity can be a blessing from God.

And what about the salvation we are all taught is coming to save us all?

The contradiction regarding the nature of salvation in the *Bible* is rooted in different passages that emphasize different elements of salvation. In some passages, such as *Ephesians 2:8-9*, salvation is said to be a gift from God that is attained through faith alone: "For by grace you have been saved through faith. And this is not your own doing; it is the gift of God, not a result of works, so that no one may boast."

However, in other passages, such as *James 2:14-17*, good works are presented as necessary for salvation: "What good is it, my brothers, if someone says he has faith but does not have works? Can that faith save him? So also faith by itself, if it does not have works, is dead."

And finally, how about Moses' statements regarding God in the *Bible*, where he describes God as a consuming fire, yet also denies that God is visible or like any visible thing. This contradiction raises questions about the reliability and consistency of religious teachings and highlights the difficulties inherent in trying to understand the nature of the divine.

The contradiction between Moses' statements about God is just one example of many that can be found in religious teachings and holy books.

Religion to Gain Power and Control

For myself, it always comes back to question of the role of religious leaders and institutions in promoting their beliefs, and the ways in which they have used religion to gain power and control over people. Below are numerous examples of how religious leaders and institutions have used religion to gain power and control over people:

The Crusades

Throughout history, religious leaders have launched crusades or holy wars to gain control over land, people, and resources. These wars were often justified by religious texts and beliefs, and were used to rally people behind a common cause. However, they resulted in widespread destruction, death, and suffering, and often had little to do with the actual teachings of the religion.

The Inquisition

The Inquisition was a powerful and often brutal institution of the Roman Catholic Church that was established in the 13th century to combat heresy. The primary focus of the Inquisition was to identify and suppress those who were believed to be heretics or apostates, and to punish them through a variety of means, including imprisonment, torture, and execution. The Inquisition began in response to the spread of heretical movements in Europe, such as the Cathars in southern France and the Waldensians in northern Italy, which were seen as threats to the authority and power of the Catholic Church.

Over time, the Inquisition grew into a vast network of tribunals, with offices and agents throughout Europe and even in the New World. In many cases, the Inquisition relied on denunciations from the general public, and often used torture to extract confessions from suspects. Those who were found guilty of heresy could be punished in a variety of ways, from forced penance and public humiliation to imprisonment and execution by burning at the stake.

The Inquisition was officially abolished by the Catholic Church in the mid-19th century, although the legacy of the institution continued to influence religious and political life in Europe for centuries. Today, the Inquisition is widely regarded as a dark chapter in the history of the Catholic Church, and a symbol of religious intolerance and persecution.

The Spanish Inquisition

The Spanish Inquisition was a brutal campaign of religious persecution carried out by the Catholic Church in Spain in the 15th and 16th centuries. Thousands of people were tortured and executed for the "crime" of not being Christian or for practicing their own religions.

Witch Hunts

Witch hunts were a phenomenon that occurred throughout Europe and North America in the 16th and 17th centuries. Religious leaders and authorities believed that witches were agents of the devil and needed to be hunted down and executed. Thousands of innocent people, mostly women, were accused of witchcraft and put to death.

The Salem Witch Trials

The Salem Witch Trials were a series of hearings and prosecutions of people accused of witchcraft in colonial Massachusetts in the late 17th century. The trials were fueled by religious fervor and superstition, with many accused witches being convicted based on hearsay and unsupported allegations. The trials resulted in the execution of

20 people and had a lasting impact on American history and culture.

Colonization and Conversion of Native Americans

The colonization of the Americas by European powers led to the forced conversion of Native Americans to Christianity. Missionaries used religious teachings as a way to control and assimilate Native Americans into European culture. This often involved the suppression of indigenous religious beliefs and practices, which were seen as pagan or heathen. The forced conversion and religious suppression had a lasting impact on Native American culture and spirituality.

Apartheid in South Africa

Apartheid was a system of institutionalized racial segregation and discrimination that was enforced by the government of South Africa from 1948 to the early 1990s. Apartheid was justified by white Afrikaner Christian leaders as a way to maintain their dominance and control over the country.

Forced Conversion of Indigenous Australians

The colonization of Australia by European powers also led to the forced conversion of indigenous Australians to Christianity. Missionaries saw indigenous beliefs as primitive and sought to replace them with Christian teachings. This often involved the suppression of indigenous spiritual practices, which were seen as pagan or heathen. The forced conversion and religious suppression had a lasting impact on indigenous Australian culture and spirituality.

The Partition of India

The Partition of India was the division of British India into two independent countries, India and Pakistan, in 1947. The partition was based on religious lines, with India becoming a secular state and Pakistan becoming an Islamic state. The partition led to widespread violence and displacement, with millions of people being forced to migrate based on their religious identity. The partition was fueled by religious tensions and was seen as a way to ensure the protection of the rights of religious minorities.

Anti-Semitism

Anti-Semitism is a form of discrimination and oppression against Jewish people. Throughout history, religious authorities have used the *Bible* to justify anti-Semitic beliefs, including the idea that Jews were responsible for the death of Jesus. This has led to numerous acts of violence against Jewish people and communities.

Religious Extremism

Religious extremism is the belief in and support of violent or extreme religious ideologies. This has led to countless acts of violence and terror throughout history, including the attacks on September 11th, 2001, and many other acts of terrorism committed in the name of religion.

ISIS

The Islamic State of Iraq and Syria (ISIS) is a terrorist group that emerged in the Middle East in the early 21st century. They have justified their violent actions, including beheadings, bombings, and mass killings, as part of their religious ideology. They claim to be fighting a holy war against those who do not follow their version of Islam.

Political Influence

Religious leaders and institutions have often wielded significant political power, using their influence to shape laws and policies that reflect their beliefs. They may endorse candidates or parties that share their views, or they may use their power to lobby for laws and policies that align with their beliefs. This can lead to the imposition of religious values on society as a whole, regardless of whether all members of that society share those values. For example, in many countries, conservative religious groups have lobbied against reproductive rights and LGBTQ+ rights, leading to the denial of basic human rights for marginalized groups.

Gender and Sexuality

Many religious institutions have been criticized for their treatment of women and sexual minorities. They may uphold patriarchal or heteronormative values, and discriminate against those who do not conform to traditional gender and sexual norms. This can have serious consequences for the individuals involved, and can contribute to broader patterns of discrimination and inequality.

Homophobia

Homophobia is discrimination and oppression against LGBTQ+ people. Many religious texts, including the Bible and the Quran, have been used to justify homophobia and to promote the idea that homosexuality is a sin. This has led to countless acts of violence and discrimination against LGBTQ+ people throughout history.

Exploitation

Religious leaders and institutions have been accused of exploiting their followers for personal gain. This can take the form of financial exploitation, such as demanding large donations or tithes, or using their positions of power to engage in sexual or other forms of exploitation. For example, in recent years, numerous scandals involving sexual abuse by Catholic priests have come to light.

Suppression of Dissent

Religious leaders and institutions have often been accused of suppressing dissenting views and punishing those who question or challenge their teachings. This can take the form of excommunication, shunning, or even violence against those who speak out. For example, during the Inquisition, many people were tortured and executed for expressing views that were deemed heretical by the Catholic Church.

Indoctrination

Religious leaders and institutions have been accused of indoctrinating their followers from a young age, instilling in them a set of beliefs that are often difficult to question or challenge. This can lead to a lack of critical thinking skills and a reluctance to question authority, which can be detrimental to both individuals and society as a whole.

Perpetuation of Social Inequalities

Religious teachings have often been used to justify social inequalities, such as gender and racial discrimination. For example, in many religions, women are barred from leadership positions and relegated to subservient roles, while people of color have been subjected to racism and discrimination in religious contexts. This perpetuates harmful stereotypes and prevents true equality and justice from being achieved.

Televangelists

In recent years, many televangelists have used religion to amass wealth and power. They often manipulate their followers by promising miracles, healing, and prosperity in exchange for donations or other forms of support. Some televangelists have been exposed as frauds, using their positions to enrich themselves at the expense of their followers.

All these examples illustrate how power-hungry individuals, religious leaders, institutions, dictators, and special interest groups can manipulate religion to gain control over people.

Not only does religion manipulate religion to control or kill people, it has also been used to divide us and create social hierarchies.

The Caste System in India

The caste system is a social hierarchy that has been in place in India for centuries. It divides people into different groups based on their birth, with the higher castes having more privileges and opportunities than the lower castes. The caste system is supported by religious texts and beliefs, which have been used to justify the discrimination and oppression of lower castes.

The Treatment of Women

Women have often been relegated to a subordinate position in many religions. Religious texts and teachings have been used to justify the idea that women are inferior to men and should be subservient to them. This has led to discrimination and oppression against women in many societies.

Religious Conflicts

Throughout history, religion has often been used to justify conflicts and wars between different groups of people. Religious differences have been used to create divisions and animosity between people, leading to violence and destruction.

Religious Persecution

Many religious groups have been persecuted throughout history for their beliefs, including Jews, Muslims, and members of various Christian denominations. This has often been due to the influence of powerful religious institutions or leaders who sought to maintain their power by suppressing opposing beliefs.

Religious Nationalism

In some cases, religion has been used to create a sense of national identity and unity, often at the expense of minority groups. This can lead to discrimination and oppression against those who do not share the dominant religious beliefs, creating a hierarchy based on religious affiliation.

In all of these cases, religion has been used as a tool to create social hierarchies and divisions between people. It has been used to justify discrimination, oppression, and violence, often at the expense of those who are considered different or inferior.

While I understand that some would argue the psychological and social functions of religion – providing examples of how it provides meaning, comfort, and a sense of community for many people. I question whether these functions could be fulfilled by other means, such as through secular humanism or other non-religious philosophies.

Alternative Belief Systems

Secular Humanism

Secular humanism is a worldview that emerged in the 20th century as a response to the growing skepticism towards traditional religious beliefs and the need for an alternative ethical and philosophical framework. At its core, secular humanism affirms the value and dignity of human life and promotes the pursuit of human happiness and flourishing through reason, ethics, and justice.

One of the central tenets of secular humanism is the importance of individual autonomy and the right to make choices based on rationality and free will. In contrast to religious dogma and divine revelation, secular humanists believe that human beings have the ability to discern right from wrong and to make ethical decisions based on empathy, compassion, and reason.

Secular humanism also emphasizes the importance of social justice and equality, rejecting discrimination and oppression based on race, gender, sexuality, or other arbitrary factors. It promotes the idea that all human beings should have equal rights and opportunities, and that society should be organized in a way that maximizes individual freedom and flourishing.

In addition to its ethical and political commitments, secular humanism also values scientific inquiry and rationality as the most reliable means of understanding the world and solving problems. It recognizes the importance of evidence-based knowledge and critical thinking and seeks to promote scientific literacy and education as a means of fostering human progress and well-being.

For those who embrace secular humanism, it can provide a sense of community and belonging, as well as a framework for finding purpose and meaning in life. It offers an alternative to traditional religious beliefs and practices, emphasizing the potential for human beings to create a better world through reason, ethics, and compassion. Ultimately, secular humanism seeks to promote the flourishing of all human beings, and to create a more just and equitable society based on shared values and ideals.

Non-religious philosophies can also offer meaning, comfort, and a sense of community.

Existentialism

Existentialism emerged in the 20th century as a response to the cultural, political, and philosophical upheavals of the time. Many thinkers felt that traditional philosophical and religious systems were inadequate for addressing the questions and challenges of modern life and turned to existentialism as a way of exploring these issues.

At the heart of existentialism is the concept of individual freedom and responsibility. According to existentialists, individuals are responsible for creating their own values and meanings in life, rather than relying on external systems or authorities to provide guidance. This means that individuals must make their own choices and take responsibility for the consequences of those choices, rather than relying on fate, God, or other external factors to dictate their lives.

Existentialists also emphasize the importance of confronting the fundamental realities of existence, such as death, meaninglessness, and freedom. By acknowledging these realities and taking responsibility for their own lives, individuals can create a sense of purpose and fulfillment that is uniquely their own.

Existentialism has been influential in a wide range of fields, including philosophy, literature, psychology, and theology. It has inspired works of literature and art that explore the themes of existentialism, such as the novels of Albert Camus and Franz Kafka, and the plays of Samuel Beckett. In psychology, existentialist ideas have been used to develop therapies that focus on helping individuals find meaning and purpose in life.

Stoicism

Stoicism is a school of philosophy that originated in ancient Greece and became popular in the Roman Empire. It teaches that individuals can achieve a state of inner calm and resilience by focusing on personal ethics and self-control. Central to Stoicism is the idea that individuals should focus on what they can control in life, such as their own thoughts and actions, and accept what they cannot control, such as external events and the actions of others.

Stoics believe that personal virtue and ethics are the highest forms of achievement and that individuals should strive to live in accordance with reason and moral principles. This involves practicing self-discipline and avoiding negative emotions such as anger and fear. By cultivating inner peace and resilience, individuals can better navigate the challenges and setbacks of life and find a sense of fulfillment and purpose.

Stoicism teaches that individuals should strive to be virtuous and live in harmony with nature, rather than pursuing material wealth or fame. It emphasizes the importance of self-reflection and introspection and encourages individuals to take responsibility for their own lives and decisions.

Stoicism has been influential throughout history and has inspired many notable figures, including the Roman Emperor Marcus Aurelius, the philosopher Epictetus, and the statesman and philosopher Seneca. It has also influenced modern psychology and psychotherapy, particularly in the areas of cognitive-behavioral therapy and acceptance and commitment therapy.

Humanism

Humanism is a non-religious philosophical and ethical worldview that focuses on the importance of human reason, ethics, and justice. It places a high value on individual freedom, human dignity, and the ability of people to make ethical decisions based on reason and empathy. Humanists believe that humans have the capacity to create their own meaning and purpose in life, and that there is no need for supernatural or divine forces to guide them.

One of the central ideas of humanism is the importance of scientific inquiry and the use of reason and evidence to understand the world. Humanists believe that the scientific method is the most effective way to gain knowledge and understanding, and they are committed to promoting science and critical thinking in society.

Another key principle of humanism is the emphasis on social justice and equality. Humanists believe that all people deserve equal rights and opportunities, regardless of their race, gender, religion, or other characteristics. They support policies and actions that promote social equality and work to eliminate discrimination and injustice.

Humanism also places a high value on personal development and self-improvement. It encourages individuals to cultivate their own talents and abilities, and to strive for excellence in all areas of life. Humanists believe that personal growth and development can lead to a greater sense of fulfillment and happiness.

In addition, humanism emphasizes the importance of community and human connection. It encourages individuals to form meaningful relationships with others and to work together to promote the common good. Humanists believe that a sense of belonging and connection to others can enhance individual well-being and promote social harmony.

Rationalism

Rationalism is a philosophical approach that emphasizes the use of reason and critical thinking to arrive at knowledge and truth. It asserts that knowledge is obtained through reason, rather than through experience or religious or supernatural beliefs. For rationalists, reason is the ultimate authority in determining truth, and skepticism and inquiry are essential to the pursuit of knowledge.

One of the key principles of rationalism is the importance of evidence and empirical data in determining the truth of a claim. Rationalists believe that all knowledge should be based on observable facts and logical deduction, rather than on subjective experience or religious revelation. This approach values the scientific method and rational inquiry as the most reliable ways of discovering truth.

Another important aspect of rationalism is its emphasis on individual autonomy and freedom of thought. Rationalists believe that individuals should have the freedom to think for themselves, without being constrained by dogma or authority. They reject the idea of blind faith and encourage individuals to critically evaluate all beliefs and claims, rather than simply accepting them on faith.

Rationalism also places a strong emphasis on ethics and morality, which are seen as natural extensions of reason and rational thought. Rationalists believe that moral principles can be arrived at through logical deduction and critical thinking, rather than relying on divine revelation or tradition. They place a high value on human dignity, freedom, and equality, and believe that these values should guide ethical decision-making.

Skepticism

Skepticism is a philosophical approach that emphasizes critical thinking, questioning, and doubt towards claims that are not supported by evidence or reason. Rather than relying on faith or authority, skeptics prioritize empirical evidence and rational inquiry in their search for truth and knowledge.

Skepticism can provide individuals with a sense of intellectual honesty and integrity, as they are encouraged to question everything, even their own beliefs and assumptions. This can lead to a more open-minded and tolerant outlook on life, as skeptics are willing to consider new ideas and perspectives.

Skepticism can also provide a sense of empowerment, as individuals are encouraged to take control of their own beliefs and decisions, rather than relying on external authorities or dogmas. This can lead to a greater sense of personal autonomy and freedom.

These philosophies can provide a sense of intellectual curiosity and fulfillment and can help individuals develop a more nuanced and complex understanding of themselves and the world around them.

Perhaps a good place to begein is to consider that religion itself is merely a construct that has been developed and used by societies to categorize and distinguish certain practices and beliefs.

What Is Religion?

I might point out that what is considered "religious" varies greatly across cultures and throughout history, and that the concept of religion has been used to justify social hierarchies and power structures.

Furthermore, the very term "religion" is problematic, as it implies a binary division between the religious and the non-religious. This division is not always clear-cut, and there are many belief systems that do not fit neatly into the category of "religion." For example, some belief systems, such as certain indigenous traditions, do not have a concept of a singular deity or a distinct separation between the sacred and the secular.

I may also invite you to question the Western notion of religion as a private, individualized practice, which is distinct from other aspects of one's life. In many cultures, religion is intertwined with politics, economics, and social life, and that it cannot be easily separated from these other aspects of society.

Finally, once you begin asking yourself the questions and reading through the evidence I present herein, you may start to believe that the concept of "religion" is a construct that has been developed and used by societies to categorize and distinguish certain practices and beliefs, and that it is not a universal or objective category. You may even find yourself calling for a more nuanced understanding of the diversity of human belief systems, and for an approach that recognizes the complex ways in which these beliefs are intertwined with other aspects of society.

In the past, religion may have played an important role in providing people with a sense of meaning and purpose in a world that was often unpredictable and difficult to understand. However, with the advancements in science and technology, we now have a better understanding of the world around us, including the quantum realities that underlie the physical universe. As a result, many people may question the relevance of religion in modern society, and whether it is still needed as a source of guidance and inspiration.

While religion may have served a valuable purpose in the past, I believe it has been supplanted by science and reason as the primary means of understanding the world. In a world where we have access to vast amounts of information and the tools to analyze and interpret it, I feel that religious beliefs and practices are outdated and no longer relevant.

However, I do also understand that religion still plays a significant role in the lives of many people, providing them with a sense of comfort, community, and spiritual guidance.

For some, the traditions and rituals of their religious faith are an integral part of their cultural identity and offer a way to connect with their heritage and ancestors. Others may find solace in the idea of a divine presence or afterlife and may turn to religion as a source of hope and comfort in times of difficulty or distress.

I ask you to consider whether these are a familial or cultural traditions or religious ones? Is it necessary to use the label of "religion" at all when we're burying our dead or eating dinner? Isn't it true that the beliefs and practices that are often categorized as "religious" could be seen simply as expressions of human experience, and that the concept of "religion" creates a false dichotomy between what is considered "spiritual" and what is considered "mundane."

These are more inclusive and open-minded approaches to exploring the diverse beliefs and practices of human societies. I encourage you to examine the underlying values and principles that inform you beliefs and practices, whether they are related to celebrating holidays, eating certain foods, or honoring your ancestors. It is important to consider how these practices can be used to promote human well-being and social justice, and to move beyond narrow religious categorizations.

By transcending the limited confines of religion and embracing a more holistic and integrated approach to exploring the human experience, you may find a deeper connection to your heritage and ancestors, and a greater sense of purpose and meaning in life. This can be achieved through a variety of means, including studying philosophy, psychology, and social justice movements, as well as engaging in personal introspection and reflection.

By focusing on shared values and principles rather than specific religious beliefs, you can foster greater understanding and cooperation among people of different backgrounds and faiths. This can contribute to building a more just and equitable society, where individuals are respected for their inherent worth and dignity, regardless of their religious affiliation.

Absurdities of Religious Belief

The Six Days of Creation

The belief that a deity created the universe in six days, as described in the *Book of Genesis*, is one of the most prominent examples of absurdities in religious belief. Despite overwhelming scientific evidence that the universe is billions of years old and the result of natural processes, some religious fundamentalists continue to cling to the idea of a literal six-day creation.

One of the major problems with this belief is that it requires a rejection of established scientific theories such as the Big Bang and evolution. These theories are supported by vast amounts of empirical evidence and have been widely accepted by the scientific community. To reject them in favor of a literal interpretation of a religious text is to reject the entire scientific enterprise.

Furthermore, the idea that the universe was created in six days is based on a very narrow and anthropocentric view of the universe. It assumes that the universe was created solely for the benefit of humans, rather than acknowledging the vastness and complexity of the natural world. This belief also ignores the fact that the universe contains billions of galaxies, each with billions of stars, and an almost infinite number of planets.

Another problem with this belief is that it is incompatible with the concept of free will. If the universe was created in six days by a deity, then that deity is responsible for every aspect of the universe, including the actions of humans. This means that any concept of free will is illusory, since our actions are predetermined by the deity that created the universe.

Additionally, the belief in a literal six-day creation ignores the rich history of cosmology and astronomy in religious thought. Many religious traditions have developed sophisticated and nuanced views of the universe, including the idea of a cyclical universe or a multiverse. By rejecting these views in favor of a literal interpretation of a religious text, believers are missing out on a wealth of religious and philosophical insights.

Finally, the belief in a literal six-day creation is often used to justify harmful and discriminatory social policies. This includes denying the reality of climate change, rejecting evolution and the science of biology, and opposing reproductive rights. These policies are often justified using religious arguments, and they can have devastating consequences for individuals and communities.

Slavery, Genocide and Violence

The belief in a literal interpretation of religious texts that condone slavery, genocide, and other forms of violence is an absurdity of religious belief. Many religious texts, including the *Bible* and the *Quran*, contain passages that seem to justify or even encourage violence against certain groups of people. For example, in the *Old Testament*, there are passages that describe the Israelites as being commanded by God to slaughter entire populations of people who were deemed to be enemies of the Jewish people.

The belief in these passages as literal, infallible truth creates a dangerous situation, as it justifies violence against other groups and can lead to dehumanization and discrimination. This has been seen throughout history, from the Crusades to the Holocaust, where religious beliefs were used to justify genocide and other forms of violence.

Moreover, the belief in literal interpretation of religious texts that condone violence ignores the historical and cultural context in which these texts were written. It fails to take into account the political, social, and economic realities of the time, and the fact that these texts were written by human beings with their own biases and agendas.

Furthermore, the belief in literal interpretation of religious texts that condone violence also fails to recognize the role of interpretation and hermeneutics in religious understanding. Religious texts are complex and often require interpretation in order to be properly understood. A literal interpretation ignores the nuances and complexities of the text and can lead to a narrow and dangerous understanding.

Additionally, the belief in literal interpretation of religious texts that condone violence can also lead to a lack of critical thinking and questioning. Instead of engaging with the text and examining it in a thoughtful and reflective way, it is simply accepted as absolute truth. This can stifle intellectual curiosity and critical inquiry, which are important aspects of a healthy and vibrant society.

Finally, the belief in literal interpretation of religious texts that condone violence can also lead to a lack of empathy and compassion for others. When a religious text is used to justify violence against a certain group, it can create a sense of "us vs. them" mentality and can lead to a lack of empathy for those who are different from us.

The All-Knowing and Powerful

The belief in an all-knowing, all-powerful deity that demands the worship and adoration of human beings is a central tenet of many religions. However, this belief raises a number of questions and concerns. One of the main issues is the apparent contradiction between the idea of a perfect and self-sufficient deity and the need for worship from humans.

On the one hand, if the deity is truly perfect and self-sufficient, then why would it require worship or adoration from humans? This seems to suggest a kind of insecurity or neediness on the part of the deity, which would be at odds with the idea of a perfect and complete being.

On the other hand, if the deity does require worship and adoration from humans, then what is the purpose or benefit of this worship? Does it benefit the deity in some way, or is it meant to benefit humans themselves? And if it is meant to benefit humans, then why is it necessary for the deity to require it, rather than simply encouraging it as a positive practice?

Another issue raised by the belief in a deity that requires worship is the question of free will. If humans are required to worship the deity, then does this mean that they are not truly free to choose their own beliefs or practices? Or, if they are free to choose, then what is the consequence of choosing not to worship the deity? Is it a moral failing, a spiritual deficiency, or something else entirely?

Furthermore, the idea of a deity that requires worship and adoration can lead to harmful or oppressive practices, such as religious coercion or the imposition of religious values on non-believers. It can also lead to a sense of superiority or entitlement among believers, who may view non-believers as somehow inferior or morally deficient.

Overall, the belief in a deity that requires worship and adoration raises a number of philosophical and ethical questions and requires careful consideration and examination. While many people find comfort and meaning in the practice of worship and devotion, it is important to approach these practices with critical reflection and an open mind, and to consider the potential implications and consequences of our beliefs and actions.

Sacrifices of Flesh and Blood

The belief that a human sacrifice was necessary for the forgiveness of sins and that consuming the flesh and blood of a divine being can bring salvation is a central tenet of Christianity. This belief is based on the idea that human beings are inherently sinful and that they require a divine intervention to be saved. According to this belief, God sent his son Jesus to die on the cross as a sacrifice for the sins of humanity. By accepting Jesus as their savior and consuming the Eucharist, believers can be forgiven and gain eternal life.

Critics of this belief argue that the idea of a human sacrifice for salvation is barbaric and unjust. They question the morality of punishing an innocent person for the sins of others and argue that it goes against the basic principles of justice. They also argue that the idea of consuming the flesh and blood of a divine being is cannibalistic and borders on superstition.

Moreover, the concept of original sin, which forms the basis of this belief, has been criticized for being inherently sexist and discriminatory. The idea that all human beings are born sinful and require salvation has been used to justify the oppression of women and the demonization of other religions and cultures.

Furthermore, the emphasis on blood sacrifice and atonement in Christianity has been criticized for promoting a culture of violence and suffering. Critics argue that the idea of a God who requires the suffering and sacrifice of his own son for the forgiveness of sins creates a framework in which violence and suffering are glorified and celebrated.

Some believers, however, argue that this belief is a fundamental aspect of their faith and provides them with a sense of hope and purpose. They argue that the sacrifice of Jesus demonstrates the depth of God's love for humanity and provides them with a path to redemption and eternal life.

The Promise of an Afterlife

The belief in an afterlife is a fundamental tenet of many religions, providing comfort to those who fear the unknown and the finality of death. However, the criteria for entering the afterlife vary greatly among different religions, often leading to arbitrary and contradictory beliefs about the nature of the afterlife.

Many religions, particularly those with an Abrahamic origin, believe in the concept of a final judgment in which individuals are judged based on their adherence to a specific moral code or belief system. For example, Christianity teaches that salvation is only possible through faith in Jesus Christ, while Islam teaches that adherence to the Five Pillars of Islam is necessary for entry into paradise.

These criteria for entry into the afterlife often result in exclusive claims by different religions, leading to conflict and division among believers. Furthermore, the concept of an afterlife based on arbitrary criteria raises questions about the fairness and justice of such a system. If a person lives a morally upright life but does not adhere to a specific religious belief, does that mean they are condemned to eternal punishment?

Another issue with the belief in an afterlife based on arbitrary criteria is the potential for coercion and manipulation. Some religious leaders may use the fear of eternal punishment or the promise of eternal reward to control the behavior of their followers, leading to abuses of power and unethical behavior.

Moreover, the belief in an afterlife based on arbitrary criteria can lead to a disregard for the present life and a focus on the afterlife instead. This can result in a neglect of important social and environmental issues, as well as a devaluing of the importance of personal relationships and human experiences.

In addition, the concept of an afterlife based on arbitrary criteria can create feelings of guilt and shame for those who are unable to meet the prescribed criteria. This can result in psychological distress and a loss of self-worth, as individuals may feel that they are not good enough to enter the afterlife.

The belief in an afterlife based on arbitrary criteria raises a number of questions and concerns about the fairness, justice, and potential for abuse associated with such a system. It is important for individuals to critically examine their beliefs about the afterlife and to consider the potential implications of such beliefs for their own lives and the world around them.

The Power of Prayer

The belief in prayer, as a means of influencing the actions of an all-knowing, all-powerful deity, is a central tenet of many religious traditions. However, this belief is also one that has been criticized for its logical inconsistencies and lack of empirical evidence.

One of the primary arguments against the belief in prayer is that it seems to contradict the very nature of an omniscient and omnipotent deity. If this deity already knows everything that is going to happen, including the actions of those who pray, then how can prayer possibly influence their actions? Moreover, if this deity is truly all-powerful, then it is difficult to understand why prayer would be necessary in the first place.

Another challenge to the belief in prayer is the lack of empirical evidence that it actually works. Despite countless studies on the subject, there is little to no evidence that prayer has any real effect on the outcomes of events or the healing of illnesses. In fact, some studies have even suggested that prayer may have a negative effect on health outcomes.

Furthermore, the belief in prayer raises difficult questions about the nature of God and the relationship between humans and the divine. If prayer is effective, does this mean that God only acts when prompted by human requests? And if so, what does this say about the supposed omniscience and omnipotence of this deity?

Critics of the belief in prayer also argue that it can lead to harmful behaviors, such as the abandonment of medical treatment in favor of relying solely on prayer for healing. This can result in unnecessary suffering and even death.

The Divine Plan: Suffering and Tragedy

The belief that suffering and tragedy are part of a divine plan or punishment is one of the most problematic aspects of religious belief. It is difficult to reconcile the existence of a loving and compassionate deity with the idea that they would allow, or even cause, pain and suffering on a grand scale. The idea that a deity would punish individuals or entire groups for perceived transgressions is also problematic, as it raises questions about justice and fairness.

The belief in a divine plan or punishment can lead to fatalism and resignation in the face of hardship, as individuals may believe that their suffering is predetermined and cannot be avoided. It can also lead to a lack of empathy for those who are suffering, as their pain is seen as part of a larger plan or punishment rather than a call to action or compassion.

Furthermore, the belief in divine punishment can be used to justify acts of violence and oppression against groups who are seen as deserving of punishment. This has been historically true of many religious groups, who have used the idea of divine punishment to justify persecution and even genocide.

The belief in divine punishment also ignores the role of natural causes and human actions in causing suffering and tragedy. Many natural disasters, such as earthquakes and hurricanes, are the result of natural forces beyond human control. Likewise, many instances of human suffering, such as poverty and illness, are the result of societal and environmental factors rather than divine punishment.

The belief in a divine plan or punishment raises significant questions about the nature of deity and the relationship between human beings and the divine. It can lead to fatalism, lack of empathy, and even violence and oppression, and ignores the role of natural causes and human actions in causing suffering and tragedy.

Eternal Damnation and Punishment

The belief in eternal damnation or punishment for non-believers or members of other religions is a core tenet of many religions. This belief holds that those who do not follow the correct religious path or belief system will face punishment or torment in the afterlife. This belief is often accompanied by a sense of superiority among believers, as they see themselves as the chosen ones who will be saved from this fate.

This belief can lead to a sense of fear and intolerance towards those who do not share the same religious beliefs. It can also lead to a lack of respect and understanding towards other cultures and religions. This belief can even be used to justify acts of violence or persecution against non-believers or those who are seen as enemies of the faith.

Furthermore, this belief raises serious ethical questions about the nature of justice and punishment. Is it justifiable to condemn someone to eternal torment simply for not believing in the "right" religion? Many argue that this belief system is both morally and intellectually flawed.

Moreover, the belief in eternal damnation can lead to a sense of guilt and fear among believers themselves. They may become obsessed with their own salvation, constantly worrying about whether they are following the correct religious path or doing enough to secure their place in the afterlife. This can lead to a narrow-minded and inward-focused worldview that neglects the needs and concerns of the wider world.

Ultimately, the belief in eternal damnation can be seen as a tool of control, used by religious leaders to maintain power and authority over their followers. By instilling fear and guilt, they can manipulate and shape the behavior of their followers, leading to a society that is intolerant, narrow-minded, and lacking in empathy towards others.

The Conspiracy of Science

The belief that scientific discoveries that contradict religious teachings are part of a grand conspiracy or deception is a common absurdity of religious belief. This belief is often held by those who adhere to a literal interpretation of religious texts and view scientific knowledge as a threat to their faith.

This belief has been perpetuated throughout history by religious authorities who have sought to suppress scientific inquiry and discoveries that contradict their teachings. For example, the Catholic Church's condemnation of Galileo for his theory that the earth revolves around the sun is a well-known example of this.

Despite overwhelming evidence to the contrary, some religious individuals and organizations continue to reject scientific discoveries in areas such as evolution, climate change, and the age of the universe. They often argue that these scientific theories are part of a grand conspiracy or deception perpetuated by atheists or other non-believers.

This belief can lead to a rejection of critical thinking and the scientific method, as well as a refusal to engage in constructive dialogue with those who hold different views. It can also prevent individuals from exploring the wonders of the natural world and gaining a deeper understanding of the universe.

Ultimately, the belief that scientific discoveries are part of a grand conspiracy or deception is a manifestation of a larger issue: the conflict between faith and reason. By rejecting scientific knowledge in favor of religious teachings, individuals who hold this belief limit their own intellectual growth and hinder their ability to fully engage with the world around them.

Nobody's Perfect

The belief that humans are inherently sinful or flawed is a common theme across many religions. According to this belief, humans are born with a sinful nature and are prone to commit immoral and sinful acts throughout their lives. This concept is often associated with the doctrine of original sin, which posits that humans inherited sin from the first human ancestors, Adam and Eve.

Many religious traditions also emphasize the importance of submitting to religious authority as a means of achieving salvation. The belief is that religious leaders have a special connection with the divine and possess the knowledge and authority to guide humans towards the path of righteousness. In some cases, the submission to religious authority is seen as a way to overcome the inherent sinful nature of humans.

However, this belief can also lead to the abuse of power by religious leaders who use their authority to control and manipulate their followers. By presenting themselves as the only means to salvation, religious leaders can coerce their followers into submission and obedience, often to the detriment of their own well-being.

Additionally, this belief can create a sense of shame and guilt among believers, as they are constantly reminded of their inherent sinful nature. This can lead to a negative self-image and a preoccupation with sin and redemption, which can detract from the enjoyment of life and the pursuit of personal growth and fulfillment.

This belief argues that it promotes a sense of helplessness and dependency among believers, as they are encouraged to rely on religious authority rather than their own personal judgment and moral compass. This can stifle critical thinking and creativity and prevent individuals from fully realizing their potential as autonomous beings.

Furthermore, the belief in the inherent sinful nature of humans can also lead to the justification of discriminatory and oppressive practices, such as the persecution of marginalized groups, based on the notion that these individuals are inherently sinful or deviant. This can create a dangerous us-versus-them mentality that perpetuates social divisions and injustices.

Chapter Two: Tensions and Disputes within Religion

I agree with the Church of England prelate's declaration that authority is the greatest enemy to truth and rational argument. In that spirit, I have written the following chapter.

Critics of Religion

The Church of England prelate who made the statement that "authority is the greatest enemy to truth" was William Ralph Inge, also known as Dean Inge. He was an English author, Anglican priest, and professor of divinity at the University of Cambridge. Inge was a prolific writer and a prominent figure in the Church of England during the first half of the 20th century. His works include *Christian Mysticism*, *Outspoken Essays*, and *The Idea of Progress*. The statement about authority being the greatest enemy to truth and rational argument is often attributed to him.

There are other historical figures within the Church of England who have made similar statements.

For example, in the 17th century, the English philosopher and bishop, John Locke, wrote that "The greatest enemy of knowledge is not ignorance, it is the illusion of knowledge," suggesting that blind faith in authority can hinder the pursuit of truth.

John Locke's statement is a reflection on the dangers of dogmatic thinking and the importance of critical inquiry in the pursuit of knowledge. He suggests that blind faith in authority or received wisdom can be a major obstacle to the acquisition of true knowledge, as it discourages people from questioning what they are told and seeking evidence to support or refute claims.

Locke's statement can be seen as a critique of religious authority, which often presents itself as the sole arbiter of truth and discourages independent thinking and questioning. Many religious traditions emphasize the importance of faith and obedience to religious leaders and texts, which can discourage critical thinking and rational inquiry.

Locke's statement is also relevant to contemporary debates over the role of expertise and authority in public discourse. In an era of increasing polarization and distrust of established institutions, there are concerns that people may be overly skeptical of expertise and scientific consensus, preferring instead to rely on their own intuitions or preconceptions.

However, as Locke suggests, blind faith in authority can be just as dangerous as blind skepticism. In order to make informed decisions and solve complex problems, we need to be able to critically evaluate evidence and arguments, and to question received wisdom and authority. This requires a commitment to ongoing learning, intellectual humility, and a willingness to engage in open and respectful dialogue with others.

Ultimately, Locke's statement is a call to recognize the limitations of our own knowledge and to embrace a spirit of intellectual curiosity and inquiry, rather than dogmatic certainty or blind faith in authority. By doing so, we can expand our understanding of the world and make more informed decisions as individuals and as a society.

Similarly, in the 19th century, the Anglican theologian and bishop, John William Colenso, challenged the traditional interpretation of the *Bible* and argued that religious authority should be subject to critical scrutiny. He famously declared, "Authority, in matters of opinion, is the greatest enemy to truth."

John William Colenso was a prominent figure in the Church of England in the mid-19th century, serving as the bishop of Natal, South Africa. He was known for his radical views on biblical interpretation, challenging traditional Christian beliefs and practices that he believed were inconsistent with reason and morality. Colenso was particularly critical of the authority of religious leaders and institutions, arguing that they often impede the pursuit of truth and progress.

Colenso's statement that "authority, in matters of opinion, is the greatest enemy to truth" reflects his belief that dogmatic adherence to tradition and authority can lead to a lack of critical thinking and inquiry. He believed that people should be free to question established beliefs and institutions, and that truth should be pursued through reason and evidence rather than blind faith. Colenso's views were controversial in his time and often earned him the ire of his fellow Anglican clergy.

Colenso's critique of religious authority was part of a broader movement in the 19th century known as biblical criticism. Scholars in this movement sought to apply critical methods of analysis to the Bible, including historical and literary analysis, in order to understand the text in its original context and to challenge traditional interpretations. Colenso was one of the most prominent figures in this movement, publishing several books on the subject that challenged the traditional interpretation of the Bible.

In addition to his views on biblical criticism, Colenso was also a vocal advocate for the rights of indigenous people in South Africa, challenging the colonialist policies of the British government and the Church. He believed that the Church had a moral obligation to support the rights and dignity of all people, regardless of their race or nationality.

The criticism of the power and authority of priests and religion, as well as the oppressive nature of their practices, is a common theme in many philosophical and intellectual traditions.

Another such critique can be found in the work of philosopher and historian David Hume, who argued that religion often relies on superstition and fear to control and manipulate people.

Hume also criticized the absurdities of ancient religious practices, such as those of the Egyptians, who believed in a pantheon of deities that were often depicted with animal heads and worshipped with elaborate rituals and sacrifices. He argued that these practices were based on mythological fables and lacked any rational or empirical basis.

Similarly, Hume was critical of modern-day religious practices that he saw as equally absurd, such as the Christian belief in transubstantiation, in which bread and wine are believed to transform into the body and blood of Jesus Christ during the sacrament of communion. He argued that this belief was symbolic and not based on any empirical evidence or rational inquiry.

Instead, Hume believed that people should be guided by natural morality, which is based on reason and critical inquiry rather than theological dogma. This approach to morality emphasizes human values such as compassion, empathy, and the pursuit of happiness and well-being for oneself and others, rather than adherence to religious commandments or traditions.

Another example is the theologian and bishop, John Robinson, who famously said in his book *Honest to God* that "The image of God as a supernatural king or lord is obsolete" and that traditional Christian language, such as that found in the creeds, had lost its meaning. Robinson argued that the Church needed to re-examine its beliefs in light of modern scientific discoveries and that religious language needed to be updated to be relevant to modern society.

John Robinson was a prominent figure in the Anglican Church in the mid-20th century, serving as a bishop and professor of theology at Cambridge University. In his book *Honest to God*, Robinson challenged traditional Christian beliefs and language, arguing that they were no longer relevant to modern society. He believed that the image of God as a supernatural king or lord was obsolete, and that traditional religious language had lost its meaning.

Robinson argued that the Church needed to adapt to the modern world and embrace new ideas and perspectives. He believed that science and technology had changed the way people saw the world and that the Church needed to incorporate these new understandings into its teachings. Robinson also believed that the Church needed to be more open and transparent in its approach, admitting that there were many things it did not know and that it could not provide all the answers.

Robinson's ideas were controversial and sparked a heated debate within the Church. Many conservative Christians criticized his views as being too liberal and a departure from traditional Christian beliefs. However, Robinson's ideas also resonated with many people who felt that the Church needed to evolve to remain relevant in a changing world.

The above statements all reflect a longstanding tension within Christianity between the authority of tradition and the search for truth through reason and critical inquiry.

Another example is Bertrand Russell, who criticized the authoritarian nature of religion and its tendency to stifle free thought and inquiry. He argued that rationality and critical thinking should be the basis of morality, rather than blind adherence to religious dogma.

René Descartes was a French philosopher who lived in the 17th century. He is known for his work *Meditations on First Philosophy*, in which he attempted to establish a foundation for knowledge based on reason alone. Descartes believed in the existence of God and that the human mind was capable of understanding the natural world through reason and logic. However, he was also skeptical of religious authority and believed that individuals should question traditional beliefs and rely on reason to discover truth. Descartes believed that religious experiences were subjective and that individuals should rely on their own reason and intuition to discern truth.

Immanuel Kant was a German philosopher who lived in the 18th century. He is known for his work *Critique of Pure Reason*, in which he attempted to reconcile rationalism and empiricism. Kant believed in the existence of God and that human reason was capable of understanding the natural world and the moral law. However, he also believed that religious beliefs were a matter of faith and that reason alone was insufficient for understanding religious truth. Kant believed that individuals should question traditional beliefs and rely on reason to discover truth, but also recognized the importance of faith and religious experience in human life.

Friedrich Nietzsche was a German philosopher who lived in the 19th century. He is known for his work *Thus Spoke Zarathustra*, in which he criticized traditional morality and religion. Nietzsche believed that religion was a product of human weakness and that it inhibited the development of human potential. He also believed that religious beliefs were a form of self-deception and that individuals should embrace life and strive for personal excellence. Nietzsche believed that reason was not sufficient for understanding human existence and that individuals should embrace their own will to power and overcome their limitations. He rejected the idea of an objective moral order and believed that individuals should create their own values based on their own experiences and perspectives.

There are also many contemporary critics of organized religion, such as Richard Dawkins and Christopher Hitchens, who argue that religion is irrational and harmful to society. They advocate for a secular, scientific worldview based on reason and evidence rather than faith.

Christopher Hitchens was a British-American author, journalist, and critic who was known for his outspoken criticism of religion and its influence on society. He was a prominent figure in the "New Atheism" movement, which sought to challenge the role of religion in public life and promote a secular worldview. Hitchens was a prolific writer, and his books such as *God Is Not Great: How Religion Poisons Everything* and *The Portable Atheist* became bestsellers. He was known for his wit and polemical style and was a frequent participant in debates and public discussions on the topic of religion.

Richard Dawkins is an English evolutionary biologist and author who is also a prominent critic of organized religion. He is best known for his book *The God Delusion*, in which he argues that belief in God is a delusion, and that religion is responsible for many of the world's problems. Dawkins is a strong advocate for science and reason and has been a vocal supporter of secularism and atheism. He is also known for his work in the field of evolutionary biology, and has authored several books on the subject, including *The Selfish Gene* and *The Blind Watchmaker*.

Both Hitchens and Dawkins have been criticized by some for their strong and uncompromising views on religion, with some arguing that they are overly dismissive of the role that religion can play in people's lives. However, they have also been praised for their contributions to the debate on the role of religion in society and their advocacy for reason and evidence-based thinking.

Karel Kosík, a Czech philosopher, was critical of religion and its role in society. Kosík was a Marxist philosopher who believed that religion was a form of false consciousness that prevented people from understanding their true social and economic conditions. He argued that religion was used by those in power to maintain their control over the masses. But note that he was a Marxist and that he taught that "religion was a form of false consciousness that prevented people from understanding their true social and economic conditions." Certainly, that fit in perfectly with his Marxist agenda.

Although speaking truth boldly may be daunting due to the power of authority, philosophers must persevere in their pursuit of truth for the sake of the few who are capable of independent thinking. Unfortunately, the majority of people are unable to discern truth as they are voluntary slaves to superstition, prejudice, and error. Hence, it is impossible to have a rational and virtuous education of youth in countries where authority enslaves people's minds.

The ecclesiastics who have an exclusive interest dominate not only the education of youth but also the consciences of old men under their control, which is supported by the false zeal and ignorance of the people. The prevalence of ignorance and folly among the masses creates an environment where crafty mystagogues can easily impose their beliefs on people, and the church flourishes so long as people believe in preternatural revelation. Although we are quick to condemn the creeds of other nations, we turn a blind eye to the absurdities in our own faith and creeds. The articles of our faith and creeds are handed down from our predecessors, and we have the title of tradition only.

I assert that all religious systems are in danger when people do not place their religion in virtue and sound morality. In such instances, the clergy would not be held in high esteem unless they promote the moral good of society. However, in cases where people believe that eternal happiness can only be dispensed by the clergy, they become the sole managers of spirituals. The highest degree of temporal advantage follows, and in almost all Christian countries of Europe, the temporal interest of the priesthood is mistaken and passes for the soul-saving spiritual interest of the laity.

Theological vs. Natural Morality

I argue that instead of teaching a theological morality, people should be taught a natural morality.

Theological morality is based on religious teachings, doctrines, and beliefs. It draws its principles and precepts from religious texts and traditions, and its adherents are expected to follow these teachings in their personal and social lives. Theological morality holds that right and wrong are determined by divine commandments, and moral values are established by religious authorities.

In contrast, natural morality is based on human reason and empirical observation. It draws on the principles of natural law and ethics, which are grounded in human nature, and seeks to establish moral values that are universally applicable to all people, regardless of their religious beliefs. Natural morality holds that moral values can be discovered through reason and critical inquiry, and that ethical behavior is a natural and rational pursuit.

This means that instead of simply interdicting vices because they are offensive to God and religion, we should prevent them by convincing people that they are destructive to their existence and render them contemptible in society. It is important to respect virtue, acquire the esteem of fellow human beings, and live a chaste, temperate, and virtuous life in order to achieve permanent felicity. These goals can be achieved without relying on religious rewards and punishments.

I also point out that the Christian world is widely divided on the religion they teach, leading to absurdities and excessive ignorance. It is clear that a state of such affairs would not be tolerated or endured amongst men, were they not compelled by the power and authority that the Church derives from its pernicious connection with the State. The clergy have imposed their superstitions upon people's minds, and whoever attacks them is punished by the civil magistrate. Despite the fact that God is the author of human reason, it is amazing that some men believe they have the right to dictate to others in matters of opinion.

Finally, I argue that the theological legends of all religions are chiefly composed of mythological fables.

Theological Legends and Myths

Theological legends are stories and myths that are often used to teach religious and moral truths to followers of a particular faith. These legends are often based on historical or spiritual events and may include supernatural or miraculous elements. However, some scholars argue that many theological legends are primarily composed of mythological fables, which are stories that have been passed down through generations and have become part of a culture's folklore.

The distinction between theological legends and mythological fables can be a subtle one. Theological legends often have a specific religious or moral message that is central to the story, while mythological fables may not have an overtly religious or moral message, but may still be used to teach important life lessons or cultural values.

For example, the story of the Garden of Eden in Christianity is a theological legend that is meant to teach the importance of obeying God's commands and the consequences of disobedience. On the other hand, the story of King Arthur and the Knights of the Round Table is a mythological fable that has been used to teach about chivalry, bravery, and loyalty.

Some scholars argue that many theological legends, particularly those that involve supernatural or miraculous elements, should be read as metaphorical rather than literal accounts of historical events. They suggest that these legends are not necessarily meant to be taken as literal truth, but rather as symbolic representations of important religious or moral concepts.

Jews copied from the Egyptians, Phoenicians, and Chaldeans, and after the second century, Christians imitated all of them in the way of parody. Therefore, it is crucial that people are allowed to think for themselves and not blindly accept the tyranny of the clergy.

Religious Imposters and God's Children

I take issue with religious impostors who promote false beliefs for their own benefit. Instead of focusing on theological teachings, I advocate for a natural morality that convinces people to be virtuous based on the benefits it brings to their existence in this world. I believe that people should be encouraged to use reason and examine matters thoroughly, rather than blindly accepting what religious leaders tell them to believe.

The majority of people remain in a state of childish ignorance due to the influence of religious leaders who promote nonsensical creeds that have no basis in reason or evidence. This pliant and passive belief system enables the church and state to dictate beliefs to people and maintain mental slavery over them. I warn that people must examine matters thoroughly and reach their own conclusions rather than allowing themselves to be told what to believe. True belief comes from a full and satisfactory conviction of the judgment and any assertion of belief without such conviction is a falsehood.

The belief that the earth is only a few thousand years old is a common idea among certain religious communities. This belief is often based on a literal interpretation of religious texts, particularly the creation stories in the *Book of Genesis*. However, the overwhelming scientific evidence suggests that the earth is much older than a few thousand years. For example, radiometric dating techniques have been used to determine the age of rocks and fossils, providing evidence that the earth is approximately 4.5 billion years old.

Despite this evidence, some religious leaders continue to promote the idea of a young earth, often claiming that scientific evidence has been misinterpreted or manipulated by secular forces. This can create a culture of anti-intellectualism and distrust of scientific inquiry, which can keep followers in a state of ignorance about scientific discoveries and advancements.

Furthermore, this belief can have real-world consequences, particularly when it comes to issues such as climate change and environmental stewardship. If followers believe that the earth is only a few thousand years old and that humans have dominion over it, they may be less likely to take action to address environmental problems or to support policies that promote sustainability.

In contrast, a worldview based on reason and evidence can lead to a deeper understanding and appreciation of the natural world, and can inspire individuals to take action to protect it. By embracing scientific inquiry and a critical examination of religious beliefs, individuals can broaden their understanding of the world and contribute to a more informed and responsible society.

Conversion therapy is a harmful practice that attempts to change a person's sexual orientation or gender identity. It is often promoted by religious leaders who view homosexuality as a sin and believe that it can be "cured" through prayer, counseling, or other methods. However, this belief is not based on reason or evidence and has been widely discredited by medical and mental health experts. The American Psychological Association, for example, has stated that conversion therapy can cause harm to individuals, including anxiety, depression, and suicidal thoughts.

Despite these warnings, some religious leaders continue to advocate for conversion therapy, keeping their followers in a state of ignorance about its harmful effects. They may promote the idea that homosexuality is a choice or a lifestyle that can be changed, rather than recognizing it as an innate aspect of a person's identity. This can lead to a dangerous and damaging cycle of shame, guilt, and self-loathing for individuals who are struggling with their sexual orientation or gender identity.

By promoting conversion therapy, religious leaders are not only perpetuating harmful and inaccurate beliefs, but they are also preventing their followers from seeking the help and support they need to live healthy and fulfilling lives. Instead, they should encourage their followers to seek out evidence-based resources and support, such as therapy and community groups, that can help them accept and embrace their authentic selves.

The belief that one's own religion or denomination is the only true path to salvation is often based on dogmatic interpretations of religious texts and the authority of religious leaders. This belief can be harmful to followers as it promotes an exclusivist and narrow-minded perspective on spirituality, which disregards the rich diversity of religious beliefs and practices around the world. This lack of openness to other religions and denominations can result in a state of ignorance and a lack of understanding of other cultures and belief systems.

Such religious leaders may teach their followers to view people of other religions as misguided or even damned, creating divisions and animosity between different groups of people. This can lead to a lack of tolerance and empathy for those who hold different beliefs, hindering the ability to work towards mutual understanding and cooperation. It can also limit personal growth and development, as followers may feel pressure to conform to a certain belief system rather than exploring different ideas and perspectives.

Moreover, the belief that only one religion or denomination is the true path to salvation can create a sense of superiority and entitlement among its followers, which may lead to discrimination, prejudice, and even violence towards those who do not share the same beliefs. This can result in the marginalization and mistreatment of people who are deemed as outsiders, leading to further social and cultural divisions.

Overall, the belief that only one religion or denomination is the true path to salvation is not based on reason or evidence and can have detrimental effects on followers and society as a whole. It is important for religious leaders and followers to embrace openness, tolerance, and respect for different beliefs and practices, in order to promote a more harmonious and inclusive world.

The Foundation of Reasoning

The foundation of all reasoning is based on self-evident truths, which are established as indisputable facts that do not require proof. These truths are the cornerstone of all knowledge and understanding and form the basis of logical reasoning. Without these fundamental truths, all attempts at persuasion and argumentation are meaningless. To convince someone of something, one must first establish these truths, as they are the foundation of all reasoning.

Unfortunately, many people are misguided by artful and interested individuals or fanatics who promote their own agenda instead of seeking the truth. The love of wealth, avarice, ease, and power creates a private interest in the priesthood, perpetuating ignorance and prejudice. The result is a system that misleads the masses with absurd and unintelligible dogmas that bear no connection to the true precepts of the Supreme Being. As a consequence, truth and honest sincerity, and consequently, goodness and virtue, are all banished.

They teach that the love of wealth and power can lead to selfish behavior and greed, often at the expense of others. Avarice is one of the seven deadly sins in many Christian traditions and is seen as a fundamental flaw in human nature. Teachings say that the pursuit of material gain and worldly pleasures can lead to a lack of concern for others and a disregard for the common good. When combined with religious authority, it can create a dangerous mix that perpetuates ignorance and prejudice.

Artful and interested individuals or fanatics often guide people, leading them to believe in ideas and beliefs that have no basis in reality. This causes confusion and misunderstanding, leading to a failure to recognize the self-evident truths that form the foundation of all reasoning. Trying to convince someone who denies these truths is pointless because they have already closed their mind to any argument based on reason and evidence.

The perpetuation of ignorance and prejudice can have dire consequences for society, leading to social and political instability, as well as human suffering. It is, therefore, crucial that we recognize the importance of self-evident truths and work to establish them as the basis of all knowledge and understanding. By doing so, we can create a world that values reason, evidence, and honesty, rather than blind faith and dogmatism.

I believe that many Mosaic accounts in the *Old Testament* are often accepted without scrutiny due to pre-instilled opinions, despite their absurdity. This can be attributed to the power of tradition and the idea that religious texts are inherently authoritative and should not be questioned. However, blindly accepting these accounts can lead to a lack of critical thinking and intellectual inquiry.

For example, the story of the Tower of Babel, in which God punishes humanity for building a tower that reached the heavens, is often accepted without question. However, upon closer examination, the story seems implausible and illogical.

Similarly, the story of Noah's Ark, in which a single family saves all of Earth's animals from a global flood, is often accepted without scrutiny, despite the many scientific and logical inconsistencies.

(Note: Mosaic accounts are stories or events recorded in the first five books of the *Old Testament*, traditionally attributed to Moses. These books include *Genesis, Exodus, Leviticus, Numbers,* and *Deuteronomy*. Mosaic accounts cover a wide range of topics, from creation and the flood to the Ten Commandments and the Israelites' journey through the wilderness. They are considered foundational to Jewish and Christian beliefs and are often interpreted as historical or theological narratives. However, as with any ancient text, there is debate and controversy over the accuracy and interpretation of Mosaic accounts.)

Atheists and Enemies

The unthinking herd of mankind often views anyone who differs from them in opinion as atheists or enemies of the Almighty Power, simply because their superstition is grounded upon the assimilation of the Supreme Being with themselves. For example, comparing Christianity with Paganism is not a sign of distrust in one's religion, but rather an attempt to understand and appreciate its true nature.

I believe that comparing different religions can be a valuable exercise in understanding the human experience. It allows individuals to gain insight into the beliefs and practices of different cultures and can help to promote empathy and tolerance.

In addition, exploring different religions can help individuals gain a deeper understanding of their own beliefs and values. By examining the similarities and differences between different religions, individuals can clarify their own beliefs and develop a more nuanced understanding of their place in the world.

Rather than seeing religion as a fixed and unchanging truth, one may view it as a dynamic and evolving human phenomenon. By approaching religion from this perspective, individuals can engage in a more open and honest dialogue about its role in society and its impact on human well-being.

Anthropomorphizing Gods

Anthropomorphizing the concept of God or a higher power is a limiting and arrogant approach that fails to appreciate the true scope and power of such an entity. By projecting human qualities and limitations onto a divine being, we reduce it to a mere extension of human thought and behavior and limit our own understanding of the universe and its workings. Moreover, the idea of a ruling power making laws that could be suspended or violated implies a certain level of fallibility and inconsistency, which is incompatible with the concept of an all-knowing and all-powerful deity. Instead, the universe operates according to immutable laws that cannot be broken or altered, and any belief to the contrary is a reflection of human limitations and biases.

This approach also raises questions about the nature of human free will and agency. If we believe that a divine being has the power to suspend or violate the laws of the universe, it implies a certain level of intervention and control over human actions and choices.

In this context, the idea of a divine being making laws that could be suspended or violated implies a certain level of limitation and fallibility, which contradicts the concept of an all-knowing and all-powerful deity. If we believe that the universe operates according to immutable laws that cannot be broken, it is logically inconsistent to assume that a higher power would create laws that are subject to change or suspension. It also contradicts the idea of individual autonomy and responsibility and reduces human beings to mere puppets or instruments of a higher power.

The concept of "God" should be understood as a divine consciousness that is beyond human comprehension yet encompasses all of creation. This consciousness is infinite and all-encompassing and can be described as the "ALL" that exists in the universe. It is not limited by time, space, or physical form. Wouldn't it be better to release the limitations on the religious construct of God and rather focus on something bigger as the "Infinite Intelligence" or the "Universal Mind."

This divine consciousness is believed to have a deep and profound understanding of all things and is characterized by infinite knowing. This means that God understands all aspects of creation, including the past, present, and future. It is this infinite knowing that allows God to guide and direct the universe in ways that are beyond human understanding.

In addition to being a divine consciousness, God is often described as the source of all creation and the ultimate reality. It is believed that all things in the universe, from the smallest particles to the largest galaxies, are connected to this divine source and that everything in creation is a manifestation of its divine energy.

The concept of God as a divine consciousness, infinite knowing, and the ALL is often associated with non-religious or philosophical approaches to spirituality, such as metaphysics or New Thought. These approaches emphasize the importance of personal growth and self-realization and encourage individuals to connect with the divine consciousness that exists within them and in the universe around them.

In this way, the concept of God transcends traditional religious beliefs and can be seen as a universal force that unites all of creation. By recognizing the true scope and power of this divine consciousness, individuals can tap into its infinite wisdom and guidance, and live their lives in harmony with the universe.

Burned and Banned

Hypatia was a prominent philosopher and teacher in Alexandria during a time when Christianity was gaining power in the region. She was known for her lectures on Neoplatonism and her critical examination of Christian theology, which challenged the early fabricators of religion.

One of the ways that Hypatia exposed the tricks of early fabricators of religion was through her emphasis on reason and critical thinking. She encouraged her students to question and examine religious beliefs and practices, rather than simply accepting them blindly. This approach challenged the authority of religious leaders and forced them to defend their beliefs with evidence and reason.

Hypatia also exposed the fallacies and inconsistencies in religious doctrines, such as the idea of a vengeful God who punishes sinners. She argued that such beliefs were based on fear and superstition, rather than reason and evidence. By exposing the flaws in religious beliefs, Hypatia paved the way for a more rational and critical approach to understanding the world and the human experience.

However, Hypatia's outspokenness and criticism of Christian theology made her a target of religious extremists. In 415 AD, she was brutally murdered by a mob of Christian zealots who accused her of witchcraft and heresy. Her death was a tragic reminder of the dangers of challenging religious dogma and the power of fanaticism to silence dissenting voices.

Despite her tragic fate, Hypatia's legacy lives on as a champion of reason and critical thinking. Her teachings and philosophy have influenced generations of thinkers and scholars, and her courage in challenging religious authority serves as an inspiration for those who seek to challenge dogma and superstition in pursuit of truth and understanding.

Giordano Bruno was a pioneer of free thought and scientific inquiry, advocating for a new, more rational approach to understanding the world. He challenged many of the established beliefs of the Catholic Church, including the geocentric model of the universe, and argued that the universe was infinite and that there were many worlds like ours. His ideas were revolutionary for his time and challenged the religious dogma that had been ingrained in Western culture for centuries.

Bruno's criticisms of the Church were not limited to scientific matters. He also questioned the authority of the Church and its interpretation of scripture, arguing that individuals should be free to interpret religious texts for themselves. He rejected the idea of a personal God who intervened in human affairs, instead seeing God as a universal force that pervaded all things.

Unfortunately, Bruno's ideas were considered heretical by the Church, and he was punished for his beliefs. He was imprisoned and tortured for years before being burned at the stake in 1600. Despite his persecution, Bruno's legacy lived on, and his ideas helped pave the way for the scientific revolution and the development of modern science.

Bruno's legacy serves as a reminder of the dangers of dogmatic thinking and the importance of free thought and inquiry. His willingness to challenge established beliefs and question authority paved the way for scientific progress and intellectual freedom. However, his tragic end also highlights the danger of challenging religious dogma in a society where religious authority holds significant power.

Baruch Spinoza was a groundbreaking philosopher who challenged traditional religious beliefs and advocated for a more rational, scientific approach to understanding the world. He rejected the idea of a personal God and instead proposed a pantheistic view of the universe, where everything is an expression of one infinite substance. This view was considered heretical by religious authorities, who saw it as a threat to traditional religious teachings.

Spinoza's works, particularly his masterpiece *Ethics*, were condemned by religious authorities and banned in many places. He was excommunicated from the Jewish community for his views and was even persecuted by secular authorities who saw him as a threat to their power. Despite this, Spinoza remained committed to his ideas and continued to write and publish his works.

Spinoza's critique of traditional religion and his rejection of dogma and superstition were groundbreaking at the time and paved the way for later thinkers in the Enlightenment period. He argued that reason and evidence, not blind faith or authority, should be the basis for understanding the world. His work was a significant contribution to the development of modern philosophy and the scientific method.

Spinoza's views were seen as so radical that they continued to be controversial and misunderstood for centuries after his death. However, his legacy as a champion of reason and scientific inquiry remains an important influence on modern thought. His ideas continue to challenge traditional religious beliefs and inspire people to seek a deeper understanding of the universe through rational inquiry.

Robert Ingersoll was a prominent figure in the late 19th century who fiercely criticized organized religion and its teachings. He was known for his lectures and writings, which advocated for a more rational and scientific approach to understanding the world. Ingersoll rejected the idea of divine revelation and argued that human reason and experience were the only reliable sources of knowledge.

Ingersoll's views on religion were considered radical and controversial for his time, and he faced significant opposition from religious authorities and conservative groups. His lectures were often disrupted by angry mobs, and his works were frequently censored or banned. Despite the obstacles he faced, Ingersoll remained committed to his mission of exposing the tricks of religion and promoting a more secular society.

In his writings, Ingersoll challenged many of the fundamental beliefs of organized religion, including the existence of God, the authority of the *Bible*, and the concept of an afterlife. He argued that these beliefs were based on myths and superstitions and had no basis in reason or evidence.

Ingersoll's criticisms of religion were not limited to theological matters. He also spoke out against the role of religion in politics and society, arguing that it had been used to justify slavery, persecution, and other forms of injustice. He believed that a secular society, based on reason and humanistic values, was the best way to promote progress and human flourishing.

Despite his contributions to the development of secular thought, Ingersoll's views were not widely accepted during his lifetime. He was often criticized and ridiculed by religious leaders and conservative groups, and his influence on broader society was limited. However, his legacy lives on, and his works continue to inspire generations of freethinkers and skeptics.

Bertrand Russell was a prolific writer and thinker who was known for his critical views on religion and its role in society. He argued that religion was based on irrational beliefs and superstitions, and that it hindered the progress of human knowledge and understanding. Russell believed that the best way to understand the world was through empirical evidence and rational inquiry, rather than relying on religious dogma or revelation.

Russell's criticisms of religion often put him at odds with the religious establishment, and his works were frequently censored and banned. He was denied teaching positions at universities due to his controversial views, and his lectures and public appearances were met with protests and opposition from religious groups.

Despite these challenges, Russell continued to speak out against religious dogma and superstition throughout his life. He believed that a more secular and humanistic approach to morality and ethics was needed, and that people should rely on reason and empathy to make moral decisions, rather than relying on religious authorities or divine commandments.

Russell's works continue to inspire and challenge readers today, and his contributions to philosophy and social thought have had a lasting impact on modern society.

Darwin's theory of evolution by natural selection challenged the traditional religious belief that all species were created in their current form by a divine being. His work posed a significant threat to the authority of religious leaders and their claims about the origins of life on earth. In particular, his theory undermined the idea of divine creation, which was a central tenet of many religious beliefs.

The opposition to Darwin's work was intense, with religious leaders arguing that it was incompatible with the teachings of the Bible and that it promoted atheism and a lack of moral values. Despite this, Darwin's theory gained acceptance within the scientific community and had a profound impact on the fields of biology and anthropology.

Darwin's ideas about evolution and the origins of life were not just a scientific theory, but a challenge to the authority of religion and its claims about the world. His work demonstrated that scientific inquiry could reveal new truths about the natural world that were not previously known or understood. As such, it posed a significant threat to religious institutions that relied on dogma and tradition rather than empirical evidence and rational inquiry.

Although Darwin himself was not persecuted for his work, his ideas were met with fierce opposition, and he faced significant backlash from religious leaders and their followers. The controversy surrounding his theory of evolution highlights the ongoing tension between religion and science and the ways in which scientific discoveries can challenge and undermine traditional religious beliefs.

These individuals challenged traditional religious beliefs and exposed the flaws and inconsistencies in religious teachings. Their works were often censored or destroyed by religious authorities who felt threatened by their ideas. Despite the obstacles they faced, these men helped pave the way for a more critical and rational approach to understanding the world.

The works of these people were destroyed or suppressed because they contained arguments that the priests could not answer. They criticized religious beliefs and practices, particularly those that they saw as irrational or superstitious. This criticism has often been met with resistance and even persecution by religious authorities, who saw such criticism as a threat to their power and influence.

In some cases, works that were critical of religion were destroyed or suppressed by religious authorities. For example, during the European Middle Ages, many works of ancient Greek philosophy were lost or destroyed because they were seen as threatening to Christian doctrine. Similarly, during the Inquisition in Spain and other parts of Europe, many books that were deemed heretical were burned or banned.

Despite this resistance, however, many philosophers and scholars have continued to speak out against religious dogma and superstition. Some have even argued that such criticism is necessary for the advancement of knowledge and the pursuit of truth.

For example, the philosopher Voltaire famously said, "Those who can make you believe absurdities can make you commit atrocities." Voltaire's statement highlights the potential dangers of blind faith and the manipulation of religious authority. According to Voltaire, when people are made to believe absurdities without questioning them, they become more susceptible to committing atrocities. In his view, the authority figures who propagate such absurdities are exploiting people's trust and exploiting the power of religious institutions for their own purposes.

Voltaire's belief is grounded in the idea that critical thinking and inquiry are essential for a healthy and just society. By questioning religious authority and scrutinizing the beliefs and practices of religious institutions, individuals can gain a better understanding of the world around them and make more informed decisions about their own lives. In contrast, blind faith can lead to ignorance and a lack of accountability, as people may be more willing to accept the actions and teachings of religious leaders without questioning their motives or methods.

This idea has been echoed throughout history by many other thinkers and leaders who have recognized the potential dangers of religious authority. By questioning absurdities and examining the motives and methods of religious leaders, individuals can make more informed decisions about their own lives and contribute to a healthier and more just society. Blind faith and acceptance of religious authority, on the other hand, can be dangerous and harmful, leading to ignorance, manipulation, and even atrocities.

The Council of Carthage

The Council of Carthage refers to several synods held in the ancient city of Carthage in North Africa (modern-day Tunisia) in the early Christian period. The most significant of these was the Council of Carthage held in 397 AD, which was attended by a number of prominent bishops from across the Western Roman Empire.

The Council of Carthage was primarily convened to discuss issues related to the biblical canon, including the inclusion of certain books in the *New Testament*. During the council, the bishops reaffirmed the traditional canon of the *Old and New Testaments* and added their official endorsement to the canonization process that had been underway for several centuries.

The council also addressed several other matters of church discipline, including the ordination of bishops, the practice of excommunication, and the treatment of heretics. It is important to note that the decisions made at the Council of Carthage were not binding on the entire Christian Church, as it was only a regional council.

Despite this, the Council of Carthage had a significant impact on the development of the Christian Church, particularly in the Western Roman Empire. The decisions made at the council were widely accepted by the bishops of the region, and the biblical canon that was endorsed by the council became the standard for the Western Church for centuries to come.

Chapter Three: Hidden Texts and Mysteries

There were many movements throughout history that challenged the Christian Church.

Challenging The Christian Church

Gnosticism is a religious movement that emerged in the 2nd century AD, characterized by its emphasis on secret knowledge or gnosis. Gnostics believed that they had access to a hidden understanding of the divine nature and the universe, which was only available to a select few who were initiated into the mysteries of the faith. This belief was seen as a direct challenge to the authority of the Christian church, which claimed to be the only legitimate interpreter of scripture and the teachings of Christ.

The early Christian church saw Gnosticism as a dangerous heresy that threatened to undermine the foundations of the faith. Gnostics rejected many of the central tenets of Christian orthodoxy, including the belief in a singular, all-powerful God, the divinity of Jesus, and the physical resurrection of the body. They also rejected the authority of the church hierarchy, seeing it as a corrupt and oppressive institution that had strayed from the original teachings of Jesus.

As Gnosticism gained popularity in the early Christian world, the church hierarchy saw it as a threat to their authority and sought to suppress it. Gnostics were often accused of spreading false teachings and leading people astray from the true faith. Many were excommunicated, persecuted, and even martyred for their beliefs.

One of the key reasons why the church sought to end Gnosticism was the belief that it was a dualistic philosophy that divided the world into two opposing forces: good and evil. This stood in contrast to the Christian belief in a singular, all-powerful God who created the world and was responsible for all that was good. Gnostics also believed in the existence of spiritual beings, or archons, who controlled the material world and were responsible for its suffering and corruption. This belief was seen as a challenge to the Christian concept of the all-powerful and benevolent God who controlled all aspects of creation.

Another reason why the church sought to end Gnosticism was the belief that it was a threat to the unity of the church. Gnostics had their own scriptures and rituals, which often differed significantly from those of the orthodox church. This led to accusations of heresy and division within the church, as Gnostics often formed their own separate communities and refused to acknowledge the authority of the orthodox church.

In the end, the church was successful in suppressing Gnosticism and establishing its own authority as the legitimate interpreter of scripture and the teachings of Christ. Many of the Gnostic texts were destroyed or lost, and their teachings were largely forgotten until the discovery of the *Nag Hammadi* library in 1945. Today, Gnosticism remains a controversial and often misunderstood religious movement, but its influence can still be felt in modern spirituality and New Age philosophy.

The Cathars

The Cathars were a Christian movement that emerged in the 12th century in southern France. They believed in a dualistic cosmology that saw the physical world as evil and the spiritual world as good. The Cathars believed that the material world was created by an evil god and that only the spiritual world could offer salvation. This belief system was in stark contrast to the orthodox Christian belief that God created the world, and that physical matter is good.

The Cathars rejected the authority of the Church and its sacraments, which they believed had been corrupted by the material world. They emphasized personal spiritual experience and direct connection to God. The Cathars believed that the Church was part of the material world and was therefore inherently evil. They rejected the sacraments of the Church, including baptism and the Eucharist, which they saw as meaningless and corrupt.

The Cathars were seen as a threat to the Church and its authority, and they were brutally persecuted. In the 13th century, the Church launched a crusade against the Cathars, known as the Albigensian Crusade, which led to the massacre of thousands of people. The Church also established the Inquisition to root out and punish heretics, including the Cathars.

Despite the persecution, the Cathars continued to spread their teachings throughout Europe. They were popular among the nobility and the middle classes, who were attracted to their message of spiritual purity and direct connection to God. The Cathars were also known for their egalitarian beliefs, which emphasized the equality of men and women and rejected the rigid hierarchy of the Church.

The Cathar movement declined in the 14th century, due in part to persecution and also to internal divisions and conflicts. However, their ideas and beliefs continued to influence spiritual movements in Europe, including the Waldensians and the Hussites. Today, the Cathars are remembered as a symbol of resistance against religious and political oppression, and their beliefs continue to inspire spiritual seekers seeking a direct connection to the divine.

The Waldensians

The Waldensians, also known as the Vaudois, were a Christian movement that emerged in the 12th century in northern Italy. The movement was founded by Peter Waldo, a wealthy merchant who renounced his material wealth and dedicated himself to preaching the Gospel. The Waldensians rejected the wealth and corruption of the Church, which they saw as an obstacle to true Christian living. They believed in a simple and humble way of life, emphasizing poverty, charity, and the imitation of Christ. They also rejected certain Church teachings, such as the doctrine of purgatory, the veneration of relics, and the idea of indulgences.

The Waldensians were known for their itinerant preaching and their commitment to spreading the Gospel to all people, regardless of social class or education. They believed in the importance of personal spiritual experience and direct contact with God, rejecting the Church's authority and sacraments. They also emphasized the importance of reading and studying the *Bible* in the vernacular, which was a radical idea at the time when Latin was the language of the Church.

The Waldensians faced persecution from the Church and secular authorities, who saw them as a threat to the established order. They were accused of heresy, and many were arrested, tortured, and killed. Despite the persecution, the Waldensians persisted in their mission, and their movement spread throughout Europe. They influenced other reform movements, such as the Hussites and the Lollards, and their ideas helped to pave the way for the Protestant Reformation.

The Hussites

The Hussites were followers of Jan Hus, a Czech religious reformer who lived in the early 15th century. Hus was critical of the Catholic Church's teachings and practices, particularly its corruption and emphasis on wealth and power. He also believed in the importance of the *Bible* as the ultimate authority in matters of faith.

After Hus was excommunicated and burned at the stake as a heretic, his followers, known as the Hussites, continued his teachings and formed their own religious movement. The Hussites rejected many of the Catholic Church's practices, such as indulgences and the sacraments, and they emphasized the importance of the Bible and individual spiritual experience.

The Hussite movement led to a series of conflicts in Bohemia, including the Hussite Wars, which lasted from 1419 to 1434. The Hussites were eventually defeated, but their ideas and teachings continued to influence religious thought in the region.

The Thirty Years' War, which lasted from 1618 to 1648, was a major conflict in Europe that was fueled in part by religious tensions between Catholics and Protestants. It began in Bohemia, where the Protestant majority rebelled against their Catholic rulers. The conflict eventually spread throughout Europe and involved many different nations and factions.

The war was characterized by brutality and devastation, with entire cities and regions being destroyed and populations being decimated. It is estimated that as many as eight million people died as a result of the war and its aftermath.

In the end, the war led to the establishment of new political and religious boundaries in Europe, with the Treaty of Westphalia granting greater religious freedom and tolerance to different faiths. The conflict also played a significant role in the development of modern nation-states and international relations.

The Lollards

The Lollards were a late medieval religious movement in England, led by John Wycliffe and his followers. They rejected many of the teachings and practices of the Roman Catholic Church, such as the idea of transubstantiation, the use of indulgences, and the authority of the Pope. They also emphasized the importance of reading the *Bible* in English, rather than Latin, so that lay people could have direct access to the Word of God.

The Lollards' views were seen as a threat to the established order and they faced persecution from both the Church and the state. Many of their leaders were arrested and executed, and their followers were marginalized and forced to practice their faith in secret. Despite this, the movement continued to spread, particularly among the lower classes and in rural areas.

The Lollards had a significant impact on the English Reformation that followed, as many of their ideas and practices were adopted by the early Protestant reformers. They also contributed to the development of the English language, as their emphasis on translating the Bible into English helped to standardize and popularize the language.

Overall, the Lollards represented a challenge to the authority of the Church and the ruling classes, as they emphasized the importance of individual conscience and direct access to God. Their legacy can still be seen in the Protestant churches that emerged in England and beyond, as well as in the English language itself.

The Protestant Reformation

The Protestant Reformation was a major movement in the 16th century that challenged the authority of the Catholic Church and led to the formation of many new Christian denominations. It was a response to the widespread corruption and abuses within the Catholic Church, such as the sale of indulgences and the political power of the Pope. The Reformers, such as Martin Luther and John Calvin, emphasized the authority of scripture and rejected certain Catholic teachings, such as the authority of the Pope and the doctrine of transubstantiation.

One of the central tenets of the Reformation was the concept of sola scriptura, or the belief that scripture alone should be the source of religious authority. This meant that the *Bible* was the ultimate authority in matters of faith and practice, rather than the teachings of the Church or its hierarchy. The Reformers believed that the Church had strayed from the teachings of the *Bible* and needed to be reformed to align with its true message.

The Reformation led to the formation of many new denominations, including Lutheranism, Calvinism, and Anglicanism. These denominations differed in their beliefs and practices, but they all emphasized the importance of scripture, faith, and personal relationship with God. The Reformation also had a profound impact on European politics and culture, leading to the rise of nation-states and the development of modern ideas about individualism and democracy.

While the Protestant Reformation challenged the authority of the Catholic Church and led to the formation of many new denominations, it also led to religious conflict and persecution.

The Wars of Religion, which lasted for over a century, were a series of wars and conflicts between Protestants and Catholics in Europe. In some cases, the conflicts were fueled by political and economic factors, but they were often driven by religious differences and a desire to protect or promote a particular faith.

Despite the conflicts and divisions that arose from the Reformation, it also had a profound and lasting impact on Christianity and Western civilization as a whole. The emphasis on scripture, faith, and personal relationship with God that emerged during the Reformation continues to shape the beliefs and practices of many Christians today.

Liberal Theology

In the 19th century, there was a growing trend among Christian theologians to move away from traditional beliefs and practices and to embrace new ideas and perspectives. This movement was known as liberal theology, and it sought to reconcile the teachings of Christianity with the advances of modern science and philosophy.

One of the leading figures in this movement was Friedrich Schleiermacher, a German theologian who argued that religious experience was the foundation of faith. Schleiermacher believed that religious experience was a feeling of absolute dependence on God, and that this feeling was the basis for all religious belief and practice.

Another important figure in the development of liberal theology was Rudolf Bultmann, a *German New Testament* scholar who emphasized the importance of historical and literary criticism in interpreting the *Bible*. Bultmann argued that many of the supernatural elements of the *Bible*, such as miracles and the resurrection of Jesus, were myths and should be interpreted symbolically.

Liberal theologians also rejected the idea of biblical inerrancy, which held that the *Bible* was without error or contradiction. Instead, they viewed the *Bible* as a historical and cultural document that reflected the beliefs and values of the people who wrote it.

Overall, liberal theology was a response to the challenges of modernity and the need to reconcile religious belief with the advances of science and philosophy. While it was controversial at the time, it has had a significant impact on the development of Christian theology and continues to influence contemporary theological discourse.

Liberation Theology

Liberation theology emerged in the 1960s and 1970s as a response to the social and political upheavals of the time, particularly in Latin America. The movement was inspired by the Second Vatican Council's call for the Church to engage more fully with the world and address social issues, and by the growing awareness of poverty and inequality in many parts of the world. Liberation theologians argued that the Church had a unique role to play in promoting social justice and working for the liberation of oppressed peoples.

The central focus of liberation theology was the idea of liberation, which referred to the struggle of the poor and marginalized for freedom from poverty, oppression, and injustice. Liberation theologians argued that the Church had a moral obligation to support this struggle and to work for social and economic justice. They rejected the traditional view of Christianity as focused solely on individual salvation and emphasized the importance of collective action and social transformation.

Liberation theology was controversial within the Catholic Church and drew criticism from some conservative theologians and Church leaders, who saw it as too political and too closely aligned with Marxist ideology. Pope John Paul II was particularly critical of the movement and sought to suppress it, although many liberation theologians continued to work within the Church and to promote their vision of social justice and liberation.

Despite its controversies, liberation theology had a significant impact on the Catholic Church and on Christian theology more broadly. It helped to shift the focus of theology from abstract philosophical and theological debates to concrete social issues and challenges, and it inspired many Christians to become more engaged in social and political activism. Today, the legacy of liberation theology can be seen in the ongoing work of social justice movements and in the ongoing efforts of Christians to address the issues of poverty, inequality, and oppression.

Overall, throughout history, there have been many movements and individuals that have challenged the authority and teachings of the Christian Church. These challenges have often led to conflict and persecution, as the Church has sought to maintain its power and influence. However, they have also contributed to the development of new ideas and perspectives within Christianity, and to a greater diversity of beliefs and practices within the faith.

The Apocrypha

The missing books of the *Bible*, also known as the *Apocrypha* or *Deuterocanonical* books, are a group of texts that were not included in the final canon of the Hebrew *Bible* or the Protestant *Old Testament*. These texts were written during the intertestamental period, between the *Old and New Testaments*, and were included in the Greek version of the *Old Testament* known as the *Septuagint*.

The books that are considered part of the Apocrypha vary between different Christian denominations, but generally include *Tobit, Judith, Wisdom of Solomon, Sirach (Ecclesiasticus), Baruch*, and *First and Second Maccabees*, as well as additions to the books of *Esther and Daniel*.

The reason why these books were excluded from the final canon of the Hebrew *Bible* or Protestant *Old Testament* is unclear and debated among scholars. Some believe that they were not originally written in Hebrew, while others suggest that they were not widely accepted by Jewish communities.

During the Reformation in the 16th century, Protestant leaders rejected the *Apocrypha*, arguing that it contained errors and lacked the divine inspiration of the rest of the *Bible*. The Council of Trent, a Catholic Church council held in the 16th century, reaffirmed the inclusion of the *Apocrypha* in the Catholic canon of the *Bible*.

Overall, the decision to include or exclude certain books in the Bible was a complex process that involved multiple factors, including questions of authorship, historical accuracy, theological consistency, and cultural context. More than likely, the teachings in these books were not aligned with the religious leaders at the time.

Perhaps you have never even heard of these books, that at one time, long ago, were part of the *Bible*.

The *Book of Tobit* is considered a deuterocanonical book, meaning it is not part of the *Hebrew Bible* but is included in the Catholic and Orthodox *Old Testament* canons. It was also included in the *Septuagint*, a Greek translation of the *Hebrew Bible* that was widely used in the early Christian Church. However, the book was not included in the Jewish canon of Scripture because it was written in Aramaic, a language not widely spoken or understood by Jews at the time. Additionally, some Jewish scholars questioned its historical accuracy and theological content. As a result, the book was not accepted into the Jewish canon and was not included in the Protestant Bible, which follows the Jewish canon.

Tobit tells the story of a righteous and pious Jewish man named Tobit. The book teaches the importance of faith, obedience, and trust in God's providence, even in times of hardship and adversity. Tobit follows the commandments of God and is a model of righteousness. He shows kindness and generosity to those in need. He also places great value on family and marriage, as seen in his desire to find a suitable wife for his son. Through Tobit's experiences and trials, the book also highlights the presence and power of divine intervention, and the ultimate victory of good over evil. Overall, the teachings of Tobit emphasize the importance of faith and virtue and provide guidance for living a life of righteousness and compassion.

The Book of Judith tells the story of a brave and cunning Jewish widow who saves her city from an invading Assyrian army. Her tale highlights the power of faith and determination, as well as the importance of using one's intelligence and resources to achieve justice and peace. Judith's character also embodies traditional Jewish values such as piety, loyalty, and courage. Despite its popularity and influence in Jewish and Christian traditions, the book of Judith is not included in the *Hebrew Bible* or *Protestant Old Testament*.

There are several theories as to why the *Book of Judith* was not included in the canon of the *Hebrew Bible* or the *Christian Old Testament*. One theory is that it was not included because it was not originally written in Hebrew, but rather in Greek, which was not considered the holy language. Another theory is that its inclusion of violent and graphic scenes, as well as its portrayal of a woman as the hero, may have been deemed too controversial or unorthodox by religious authorities.

The *Wisdom of Solomon* is a book in the *Apocrypha*, which is a collection of texts that were not included in the canon of the *Hebrew Bible* or the *Christian New Testament*. It is also sometimes referred to as the *Book of Wisdom*.

The *Wisdom of Solomon* is a philosophical and poetic work that was likely written in Alexandria, Egypt, during the 1st century BCE or the 1st century CE. It explores themes such as wisdom, righteousness, and the immortality of the soul, and it draws on Jewish and Hellenistic Greek traditions.

One reason why the *Wisdom of Solomon* may have been excluded from the canon of the Bible is because it was not originally written in Hebrew, which was the language of the Jewish scriptures. Instead, it was written in Greek, which was the language of the Hellenistic world.

Additionally, some Christian theologians were uncomfortable with some of the philosophical ideas expressed in the *Wisdom of Solomon*. For example, the book describes wisdom as a feminine and divine figure, which may have conflicted with traditional Christian beliefs about the nature of God.

Sirach, also known as *Ecclesiasticus*, is a book of the *Old Testament* that was written by the Jewish scribe Shimon ben Yeshua ben Eliezer ben Sira in the early 2nd century BCE. It is a collection of wisdom sayings and moral teachings, and it was widely read and respected in the Jewish community.

However, the *Book of Sirach* was not included in the Jewish canon of scripture, and it was not included in the *Protestant Bible*. The Catholic and Orthodox Churches did include it in their canons, but it was considered deuterocanonical, meaning that it was not considered part of the core canon.

There are several reasons why *Sirach* may not have been included in the canon of scripture. One reason is that it was written relatively late, after the major prophets of the *Old Testament*. Additionally, the book was written in Hebrew, but the earliest surviving copies are in Greek, which may have made it less authoritative to Jewish scholars.

Another reason why *Sirach* may not have been included in the canon is that some of its teachings are seen as controversial or at odds with other Jewish writings. For example, *Sirach* emphasizes the importance of wisdom and obedience to the law, but it also includes teachings about the role of women and the value of celibacy that are not found in other Jewish texts. The *Book of Sirach* contains passages that reflect the patriarchal values of its time. For example, *Sirach* teaches that a woman's role is primarily in the domestic sphere and that her value is often tied to her ability to bear children and fulfill the needs of her husband.

The Book of Baruch is a deuterocanonical book of the Old Testament, meaning it is considered canonical by some Christian denominations but not by others. It is not included in the Jewish Bible. The book is attributed to Baruch, the scribe of the prophet Jeremiah.

The *Book of Baruch* consists of five chapters and is primarily concerned with the Babylonian exile and the eventual return of the Jewish people to their homeland. It includes a prayer of confession and a prayer for mercy, as well as a prophecy of the future redemption of Jerusalem.

One reason why *Baruch* may not have been included in the *Hebrew Bible* is its inclusion of ideas that were not in line with mainstream Jewish thought.

The *Letter of Jeremiah*, also known as the *Epistle of Jeremiah*, is a short book in the *Old Testament Apocrypha*. It is attributed to the prophet Jeremiah and consists of a letter that he supposedly wrote to the Jews who were taken captive to Babylon.

The letter is primarily concerned with denouncing the worship of idols and the practice of making and worshiping statues. It describes the futility of idol worship and how idols are made by human hands and cannot hear or answer prayers. The letter urges the Jews to turn away from idolatry and to follow the commandments of God.

First and Second Maccabees are two books that provide an account of the Jewish revolt against the Seleucid Empire in the 2nd century BCE. The books tell the story of the Maccabean family, who led the rebellion and reestablished Jewish worship in Jerusalem.

Although the books were considered important historical records by early Christian communities, they were not included in the *Hebrew Bible*, which was compiled before the events described in the books took place.

In the Christian tradition, the books were included in the *Old Testament Apocrypha*, a collection of religious texts that were not considered part of the official canon but were still considered valuable for religious and moral instruction. However, during the Protestant Reformation, these books were removed from the *Bible* by Protestant reformers, who believed that they did not carry the same authority as the books of the Hebrew canon.

The *Additions to the Book of Esther* are a series of texts that were originally included in the Greek version of the *Book of Esther* but were later removed from the Hebrew version of the *Old Testament*. These additions include the Greek version of Esther's prayers, as well as additional stories and verses that are not present in the Hebrew text.

The reason why the *Additions to the Book of Esther* were removed from the Hebrew version of the *Old Testament* is not entirely clear, but it may be due to the fact that they were not part of the original Hebrew text and were written in Greek. Additionally, some of the additions contain religious themes and motifs that are not present in the Hebrew version and may have been seen as inconsistent with Jewish beliefs and practices.

One of the most notable additions to the *Book of Esther* is the character of Mordecai, who is depicted as a hero and leader in the Greek text. The Greek version also includes a prayer by Esther in which she asks for God's help in saving her people from their enemies, which is not present in the Hebrew text.

Additions to the *Book of Daniel*, including the *Prayer of Azariah*, the *Song of the Three Young Men*, and the story of *Susanna and the Elders*, as well as the longer version of the *Book of Daniel*.

The story of *Susanna and the Elders* is a tale from the Greek version of the *Book of Daniel* that recounts the plight of a virtuous woman named Susanna who is falsely accused of adultery by two wicked elders.

According to the story, Susanna is a beautiful and pious woman who lives in Babylon with her wealthy husband. One day, while she is bathing in her garden, two elders who are spying on her confront her and demand that she have sex with them or else they will accuse her of adultery with a young man. Susanna refuses their advances and the elders carry out their threat, falsely accusing her of adultery before the people.

Susanna is brought before a court to be tried for her alleged crime, but with the help of the young prophet Daniel, she is able to prove her innocence by exposing the elders' lies and contradictions. The elders are then put to death for their wickedness, and Susanna is acquitted and allowed to live in peace.

Do you see why some of these books were removed? I see themes of women having agency and power in some of the excluded texts, which may have been considered controversial or threatening in the patriarchal societies that existed at the time. These texts challenged traditional gender roles and undermined the authority of male leaders within religious communities. Additionally, some of the excluded texts were seen as promoting ideas or practices that were not in line with the dominant religious ideology of the time and were therefore excluded from the canon.

The Gospel of Judas is a Gnostic gospel that provides a different perspective on the story of Jesus Christ and his disciples. It was discovered in the 1970s in Egypt, but its existence was only made public in 2006. The gospel consists of 26 pages, and its content suggests that the character of Judas Iscariot may have been misunderstood in the traditional Christian narrative. In the gospel, Judas is portrayed as a trusted disciple who was chosen by Jesus to carry out a secret mission.

According to the gospel, Jesus tells Judas that he will be blessed if he betrays him, as it will allow Jesus to fulfill his divine mission. The text suggests that Judas did not act out of greed or malice but was simply following Jesus' instructions. This portrayal of Judas differs significantly from the traditional view, where he is typically viewed as a traitor who sold out Jesus for thirty pieces of silver.

The Gospel of Judas also reflects Gnostic beliefs, which were popular in the early Christian era but were eventually suppressed by the Church.

Despite its potential significance, *The Gospel of Judas* was not included in the *Bible* and was considered heretical by the early Church. The text was likely excluded because it contradicted traditional Christian beliefs about how and where to seek God, about the actual character of Judas, and the events surrounding the crucifixion of Jesus.

The Acts of Paul and Thecla is a fascinating early Christian text that has been deemed controversial because of its progressive portrayal of women. The story revolves around a young woman named Thecla, who falls in love with the teachings of Paul, one of the apostles of Jesus Christ. Despite the opposition of her family and the patriarchal society in which she lived, Thecla converts to Christianity and becomes an ardent follower of Paul.

The text portrays Thecla as a strong and virtuous woman who performs many miracles in the name of Jesus. She heals the sick, drives out demons, and even tames wild beasts with her faith. Thecla's unwavering commitment to her faith and her willingness to suffer martyrdom for her beliefs are held up as examples of true Christian devotion.

However, it is Thecla's leadership role in the early Christian church that caused controversy. The text describes how Thecla is ordained as a deaconess by Paul and given the authority to preach and baptize. This portrayal of a woman in a position of power within the church challenged the patriarchal norms of early Christianity and was seen as a threat to the established order.

Despite this controversy, *The Acts of Paul and Thecla* was widely read and influential in the early Christian church. It was even included in some early versions of the *New Testament*, although it was eventually excluded from the canon of scripture due to its unorthodox teachings about women's roles in the church.

The Apocalypse of Peter is an early Christian text that depicts a journey through hell and the afterlife. It is a vivid and graphic description of the punishments that await sinners in the afterlife, including the damned being thrown into fiery pits, tortured by demons, and suffering indescribable torments. The text also describes the fate of the righteous and their eventual ascent to heaven.

The Apocalypse of Peter was considered controversial because it presented a different view of the afterlife than the traditional Christian view. It portrays a more vivid and gruesome version of hell and the torments of sinners. Some early Christian leaders believed that the text was too disturbing and graphic for general consumption and that it could lead to a misunderstanding of Christian beliefs about the afterlife. As a result, the text was not included in the official canon of the *New Testament*, but it remained popular among some Christian communities and has influenced later works of literature, including Dante's *Divine Comedy*.

The Epistle of Barnabas is a text that is attributed to the early Christian leader Barnabas, who was a companion of the apostle Paul. The text is thought to have been written in the late first or early second century, and it offers a commentary on the *Old Testament* that emphasizes the idea that Christians are the true heirs of the Jewish faith. In particular, the text argues that the Jewish law was only a temporary measure and that it has been superseded by the new covenant established by Jesus Christ.

One of the main reasons why *The Epistle of Barnabas* was considered controversial is because it argued against the observance of Jewish law. This was a particularly sensitive issue in the early Christian church, as there were many Jewish converts who wanted to continue observing the law. *The Epistle of Barnabas* argues that the Jewish law was only a shadow of the true law, which was revealed in Christ. Christians are now bound by a new law, which is the law of love.

Another reason why *The Epistle of Barnabas* was controversial is because it promotes the idea of allegorical interpretation of the *Old Testament*. The *Old Testament* contains hidden meanings that can only be understood through allegory. This was a departure from the more literal interpretation of the *Old Testament* that was common at the time, and it was seen by some as a threat to the authority of scripture.

Despite its controversial nature, *The Epistle of Barnabas* was widely circulated in the early Christian church and was even considered for inclusion in the *New Testament* canon. However, it was ultimately not included, perhaps due to its controversial teachings on Jewish law and allegorical interpretation. Nevertheless, the text remains an important example of early Christian thought and provides valuable insight into the development of Christian theology in the first centuries after Christ.

The Shepherd of Hermas is a fascinating early Christian text that was highly regarded in the early church but ultimately not included in the canon of the *New Testament*. The text is composed of a series of visions and parables, delivered to a man named Hermas by an angelic figure who serves as his guide. The overarching message of the text is one of ethical living and repentance, with a particular emphasis on the need for forgiveness and the possibility of redemption even after sin has been committed.

One of the most controversial aspects of *The Shepherd of Hermas* was its treatment of the idea of post-baptismal repentance. At the time the text was written, there was a significant debate within the early church about whether it was possible to be forgiven of sins after baptism. Some church leaders believed that baptism was a one-time event that conferred permanent forgiveness, while others argued that it was possible to be forgiven of sins committed after baptism through repentance and confession.

The Shepherd of Hermas took a middle ground on this issue, suggesting that while baptism was indeed a powerful sacrament that conferred significant grace, it was still possible to fall into sin and that repentance was a necessary step towards restoration. This message was controversial because it challenged the prevailing view of some church leaders and offered a more compassionate and forgiving approach to the issue of sin and redemption.

Overall, *The Shepherd of Hermas* offers a unique perspective on early Christianity, emphasizing the importance of ethical living and the possibility of repentance and redemption even after sin has been committed. While the text was ultimately not included in the *New Testament* canon, it remains an important and influential work in the history of Christianity.

The story of *Bel and the Dragon* tells the story of Daniel exposing the fraud of the priests of Bel and the dragon, two pagan idols. The king, who had been tricked into believing in the power of these idols, orders that Daniel be thrown into a den of lions. However, God protects Daniel, and he survives unharmed. The story was not included in the *Hebrew Bible*, and later, the *Protestant Bible*, likely because it was seen as too strongly promoting monotheism and challenging the power of pagan gods.

Monotheism is the belief in the existence of one single deity or god. It is the opposite of polytheism, which is the belief in multiple gods or deities. Monotheistic religions include Judaism, Christianity, and Islam, among others. These religions teach that there is only one God who is all-knowing, all-powerful, and who created the universe. Monotheism emphasizes the unity and oneness of God and encourages a personal relationship between the individual and the divine.

1 Esdras and *2 Esdras* (also known as *4 Ezra*) are two apocryphal books that were excluded from the *Bible*. *1 Esdras* is considered to be a historical text, providing an account of the rebuilding of the temple in Jerusalem after the Babylonian captivity. It also includes stories from the book of Ezra and

Nehemiah, as well as additional stories not found in the *Bible*.

2 Esdras, on the other hand, is a Jewish apocalyptic work that is also known as *4 Ezra*. It contains visions and prophecies given to the prophet Ezra and includes themes such as the end of the world, the final judgment, and the afterlife. It also contains a discussion about the nature of free will and predestination.

Both *1 Esdras* and *2 Esdras* were excluded from the Bible for various reasons, including questions about their authorship and authenticity, and concerns about their doctrinal consistency with the rest of the biblical canon.

The Psalms of Solomon is a collection of 18 hymns and prayers that were composed in Hebrew and later translated into Greek. They were likely written by a Jewish author or group of authors between the 1st century BCE and the 1st century CE, and they reflect the political and religious tensions of the time.

The Psalms of Solomon were not included in the *Hebrew Bible* or the *Christian Old Testament*, but they were highly influential in early Christian literature and worship. They were often quoted or alluded to by early Christian writers, including Paul the Apostle and Justin Martyr.

The Psalms of Solomon are notable for their emphasis on the coming of a messianic figure who will bring justice and peace to Israel. This figure is described as a king and a priest, who will lead a rebellion against foreign oppressors and establish a righteous kingdom on earth.

The Psalms of Solomon were likely excluded from the Bible because they were not considered to be part of the Hebrew canon, and because they contained some teachings and beliefs that were not in line with mainstream Jewish or Christian thought.

The Odes of Solomon is a collection of 42 hymns and poems that were likely written by an early Christian poet in Syria. They date back to the 2nd century CE and are considered to be one of the earliest examples of Christian hymnody.

The Odes of Solomon were not included in the canon of the Bible for a number of reasons. First, they were not widely circulated and were not as well-known as other Christian texts at the time. Second, the *Odes* contain mystical and esoteric themes that may have been seen as too abstract or difficult for the average Christian to understand. Third, the *Odes* contain a strong emphasis on personal spiritual experience and direct communion with God, which may have been seen as a threat to the authority of the institutional church.

The Infancy Gospel of James is an early Christian text that dates back to the second century CE. It is also known as the *Protoevangelium of James* and tells the story of the life of Mary, the mother of Jesus. The text describes Mary's miraculous birth, her upbringing in the temple, and her marriage to Joseph. It also includes details about the birth of Jesus and his early life.

The Infancy Gospel of James was excluded from the Bible because it contained several stories that were not found in the canonical Gospels and contradicted some of the accepted Christian teachings. For example, the text describes Mary's virginity as perpetual, which was not a widely accepted belief in the early Christian church. Additionally, the text includes stories about Jesus performing miracles as a young child, such as healing a blind man, which were not included in the canonical Gospels.

Furthermore, some of the stories in *The Infancy Gospel of James* were seen as promoting a view of Christianity that was considered heretical by the church leaders. For example, the text describes Mary as being sinless, which contradicts the doctrine of original sin. The text was also seen as promoting the idea of salvation through good works, rather than through faith alone, which was a controversial idea in the early Christian church.

The Infancy Gospel of Thomas is a text that tells the story of Jesus as a child, and includes various miraculous events and episodes of Jesus displaying his divine powers. The text was excluded from the *Bible* because it was believed to have been written much later than the canonical gospels, and because it contained many fantastical and implausible stories.

Additionally, some of the stories in *The Infancy Gospel of Thomas* were seen as contradictory to the character and teachings of Jesus in the canonical gospels, and some of the actions of young Jesus were seen as disrespectful or even cruel.

The Acts of Peter is an early Christian text that tells the story of the apostle Peter and his ministry. The text includes various accounts of miracles performed by Peter, as well as his teachings on morality and ethics. However, the text was considered controversial by some Christian authorities due to its inclusion of certain elements that were seen as heretical or non-canonical. For example, the text includes descriptions of Peter's encounters with a woman named Sophia, who is depicted as a spiritual leader and miracle worker. This portrayal of a woman in a leadership role was seen as subversive by some early Christian leaders who sought to establish a more patriarchal hierarchy. As a result, *The Acts of Peter* was ultimately excluded from the canon of the New Testament.

The Acts of Paul is a set of texts that describe the travels and teachings of the Apostle Paul, as well as his persecution and eventual martyrdom. The texts include stories of miraculous events and encounters with supernatural beings. They also feature prominent female characters, such as Thecla, who plays a significant role in Paul's ministry.

The Acts of Paul was considered controversial by some early Christian leaders, as it promoted the idea of women in leadership roles and challenged traditional views on marriage and celibacy. In addition, some scholars argue that *The Acts of Paul* contain elements of Gnosticism, a set of beliefs considered heretical by many early Christian leaders.

The Acts of John is an early Christian text that was likely written in the second century AD. It tells the story of the apostle John and his travels, miracles, and teachings. The text includes several accounts of John raising people from the dead, healing the sick, and performing other miracles. It also features a mystical account of John's vision of Jesus and his teachings on the nature of God and the universe.

The Acts of John was widely read and revered in the early Christian Church, but it was eventually excluded from the canon of scripture due to its controversial teachings and mystical content. Some of its teachings, such as the idea that Jesus did not physically die on the cross, were considered heretical by the church authorities.

Additionally, the text's emphasis on personal revelation and spiritual experience over institutional authority clashed with the emerging structures of the organized church. Despite its exclusion from the canon, *The Acts of John* remained influential in Christian mysticism and Gnostic circles.

The Acts of Andrew is an apocryphal text that tells the story of Andrew, one of the twelve apostles of Jesus. It describes his travels and missionary work in various parts of the world, including Scythia (modern-day Ukraine), Greece, and Asia Minor. The text also recounts many miracles performed by Andrew and describes his eventual martyrdom by crucifixion.

The Acts of Andrew is not included in the canon of the *New Testament*, nor in the *Old Testament*. It is considered one of the apocryphal Acts of the Apostles and was likely written in the 2nd or 3rd century. The reasons for its exclusion from the canon may be due to its legendary and fantastical elements. Did the church want mere men performing miracles?

The Shepherd of Hermas is a text from the 2nd century that uses visions and parables to encourage ethical living and repentance. The text was considered controversial because it suggested that repentance was possible after baptism, which was contrary to the views of some church leaders. Additionally, some of the teachings in the text contradicted the doctrines of the established church, particularly with regard to the nature of Christ and the concept of free will. As a result, the Shepherd of Hermas was excluded from the canon of scripture in many early Christian communities.

The Epistle of Barnabas is a text that was written in the early Christian period, likely in the late first or early second century CE. It is an early Christian apologetic work that offers commentary on the *Old Testament* and emphasizes the idea that Christians are the true heirs of the Jewish faith. The text was considered controversial because it argued against the observance of Jewish law, and because it advocated for a highly allegorical interpretation of the *Bible*.

The Didache is a Christian document from the first century that provides practical instructions for Christian communities. It covers topics such as baptism, fasting, prayer, and the Eucharist, as well as ethical teachings on topics like honesty, love, and humility. Despite being a widely used and respected text in the early Christian church, it was eventually excluded from the Bible and not included in the canon of scripture.

The reasons for this exclusion are not entirely clear, but some scholars suggest that it may have been due to its emphasis on practical instruction rather than theological doctrine, or because it was not widely circulated or accepted outside of certain regions.

In this context, practical instruction refers to guidance or advice on how to live or act in a particular way, often with a focus on specific actions or behaviors. It is more concerned with practical matters and can include things like moral or ethical principles, instructions for religious practices, or guidance for social interactions.

On the other hand, theological doctrine refers to beliefs or teachings about the nature of God or the divine, the universe, and humanity. It is more concerned with abstract concepts and ideas, such as the nature of sin, redemption, salvation, and the afterlife. Theological doctrine often involves the interpretation of religious texts and the development of philosophical and theological frameworks to explain and understand these beliefs.

Mary Magdalene and Thomas

*The Apocryphal Gospel of the Nativity of Mary,
The Gospel of Mary Magdalene* and the *Gospel of
Thomas* are most likely the most discussed among
the texts that were not included in the biblical
canon because they were not widely accepted by
early Christian communities or were deemed
heretical by some church leaders.

The Apocryphal Gospel of the Nativity of Mary is a
non-canonical gospel that tells the story of the birth
and early life of Mary, the mother of Jesus. The
gospel is believed to have been composed in the
late second century or early third century AD and
is part of a larger collection of texts known as the
New Testament Apocrypha.

According to the gospel, Mary's parents, Joachim
and Anna, were barren and unable to conceive a
child. After much prayer and fasting, an angel
appeared to Joachim and announced that Anna
would conceive a child. Anna gave birth to Mary
and dedicated her to the service of God at a young
age.

According to the apocryphal *Gospel of the Nativity
of Mary*, Mary was consecrated to the Lord at a
young age and brought up in the temple. This has
led to the suspicion that her pregnancy was the
result of an intrigue with the priests who convinced
her that it was God who had fathered her child.

The high priest was likely the main figure in this plot and chose Joseph, an elderly man who had previously been married and had six children, to be Mary's husband. *The Gospel of James* declares that Joseph married Mary, but did not consummate the marriage.

The gospel also includes stories about Mary's childhood, including her education and her betrothal to Joseph. It describes how Mary was chosen to bear the Son of God and how she was visited by the angel Gabriel, who announced to her that she would conceive a child by the Holy Spirit.

The Apocryphal Gospel of the Nativity of Mary is not considered to be part of the canon of Scripture and is not included in most modern editions of the Bible. However, it is still studied and read by some scholars and religious communities as an important source of information about the life and times of Mary and the early Christian church.

The Gospel of Mary Magdalene is an early Christian Gnostic text that was discovered in the late 19th century in Egypt. The text, which is believed to have been written in the 2nd century, portrays Mary Magdalene as a visionary and leader among Jesus' disciples. In this gospel, Mary Magdalene is presented as a prominent disciple who received special teachings from Jesus and who was entrusted with a secret revelation.

The gospel begins with Mary Magdalene weeping outside Jesus' tomb, and then goes on to describe a dialogue between Mary Magdalene and the other disciples, in which she relates her visionary experience of encountering the risen Christ. The text also includes teachings by Jesus, in which he emphasizes the importance of inner spiritual development and knowledge of oneself.

The Gospel of Mary Magdalene is a valuable historical document that sheds light on the early Christian movement and its diversity of beliefs and practices. Its portrayal of Mary Magdalene as a prominent disciple challenges the traditional view of her as a repentant sinner and highlights the significant role that women played in the early Christian movement.

Some scholars argue that the text was written by Mary Magdalene herself, while others suggest that it was written by a member of her community. Regardless of its origins, the text provides valuable insights into the diverse range of beliefs and practices that existed within the early Christian movement.

The Gospel of Thomas is a collection of sayings attributed to Jesus himself, that emphasizes the importance of individual spiritual seeking and insight.

The Gospel of Thomas is a non-canonical text believed to have been written in the early second century. It is a collection of sayings, or logia, attributed to Jesus, without any narrative or biographical content. The text is part of the *Nag Hammadi* library, discovered in Egypt in 1945, which includes several Gnostic texts.

The Gospel of Thomas emphasizes many sayings attributed to Jesus that emphasize the importance of self-knowledge and inner spiritual growth over blind adherence to external dogma or tradition.

In this context, Jesus is presented as a teacher who encourages his followers to look within themselves to discover the divine spark that exists within each person. Rather than relying on external authorities or institutions to define their faith, Jesus suggests that individuals should cultivate a direct, personal relationship with God or the divine through prayer, meditation, and self-reflection.

This emphasis on self-knowledge and inner spiritual growth is also reflected in other aspects of the text, such as its emphasis on the role of the individual in spiritual transformation and its rejection of hierarchical structures and authority figures in favor of a more egalitarian and decentralized approach to religious practice.

The sayings in *The Gospel of Thomas* are often cryptic and open to interpretation, but they generally promote a message of inner spiritual development, personal transformation, and the attainment of higher consciousness. Some of the sayings express a mystical and esoteric understanding of the nature of reality, suggesting that the world is an illusion and that the true nature of existence can only be grasped through spiritual insight.

The Gospel of Thomas was likely written by a group of Gnostic Christians who believed in the importance of direct personal revelation and spiritual insight, rather than relying on external authorities or institutions. The text offers a unique perspective on the teachings of Jesus and provides insight into the spiritual beliefs and practices of a group of early Christians who were outside the mainstream of the church.

The exclusion of these books from the canon of scripture may have been due to various reasons, including their potential to challenge established theological beliefs, and their association with groups that were considered heretical or outside of the mainstream of religious thought. It is also possible that these texts were excluded because they contained ideas that were too progressive or not aligned with the dominant teachings of the time.

Religious institutions have historically sought to exert control over their followers and maintain their authority through the dissemination of carefully curated teachings and texts. In this context, any ideas or teachings that challenged the status quo or deviated from established doctrines may have been seen as threatening to the power of the religious institutions.

Moreover, the process of canonization itself involved a degree of censorship and editing, as religious leaders and scholars sought to determine which texts would be included in the official canon of scripture. In this process, some texts may have been excluded because they did not align with the theological and political objectives of the religious authorities.

Overall, the exclusion of certain books from the canon of scripture may reflect the power dynamics and politics of the time, as well as the desire of religious institutions to control and shape the beliefs and practices of their followers.

Miracles

I argue against the existence of miracles as they contradict nature, reason, and experience. It is more likely that stories of miracles were propagated by people who lived thousands of years ago, rather than the actual occurrence of supernatural events. The human mind has a tendency to be taken by surprise and commit to things it does not fully comprehend, such as supernatural events. This has led to the perpetuation of miracle stories throughout history, despite the lack of evidence to support them.

It is important to rely on reason and evidence when considering claims of miracles. In many cases, there are natural explanations for events that may appear miraculous at first glance.

The growth of miracles seems to be most abundant in the *Old Testament*, and yet, if these stories appeared in the writings of a Grecian philosopher or an early Mahometan, they would be met with scorn and sarcasm. This is due to the early impression that Moses had heavenly inspirations.

Those who disagree with these views are often labeled as atheistic or heretical without fully understanding the true nature of atheism. Atheism involves the denial of an Almighty Power ruling the universe or its benevolent providence and does not necessarily imply an absence of morality or ethics.

The uncritical acceptance of Mosaic accounts and miracles perpetuates a culture of blind faith and discourages critical thinking and inquiry. This can be dangerous, as it allows for the perpetuation of harmful or oppressive beliefs and practices under the guise of religious authority.

As a result, it is essential to approach religious texts and beliefs with a critical and discerning eye, evaluating them based on reason and evidence rather than blindly accepting them due to preconceived notions or religious authority.

Ultimately, the goal should be to foster a culture of open inquiry and intellectual honesty, where beliefs and ideas can be examined and scrutinized without fear of persecution or condemnation. This can lead to a more robust and nuanced understanding of religion and its place in the world and can promote greater respect and understanding among individuals of different faiths and worldviews.

The number of miracles in the *Old Testament* is difficult to quantify, as it depends on how one defines a miracle. Some scholars argue that every supernatural event in the *Old Testament* could be considered a miracle, while others take a narrower view and only count certain events as miracles.

Jesus' Miracles

In Christianity, miracles are believed to be supernatural events that cannot be explained by natural or scientific laws and are attributed to the divine intervention of God. The *Bible* describes numerous miraculous events attributed to Jesus, such as healing the sick, feeding the multitude with a few loaves of bread and fish, calming the storm, and even raising the dead.

One of the most well-known miracles is the turning of water into wine at a wedding feast in Cana, which is described in the *Gospel of John*. According to the story, Jesus turned water into wine when the hosts of the wedding ran out of wine, which was seen as a sign of his divine power and authority.

Another miracle attributed to Jesus is walking on water, which is described in *the Gospels of Matthew, Mark,* and *John.* According to the story, Jesus walked on water to meet his disciples who were in a boat, and when they saw him, they were frightened, thinking he was a ghost. Jesus reassured them, and Peter even attempted to walk on the water himself, but he began to sink and Jesus saved him.

The raising of the dead is another miracle attributed to Jesus, and it is described in the *Gospels of Mark, Luke*, and *John.* According to the story, Jesus raised several people from the dead, including Lazarus, a man who had been dead for four days. These miraculous events were seen as evidence of Jesus' divine nature and his power over death, and they played an important role in his teachings and the spread of Christianity.

There is no physical or scientific evidence that Jesus actually turned water into wine. Nor is there any modern scientific evidence to support the idea of turning water into wine. The laws of physics and chemistry do not allow for such a transformation to occur naturally or artificially. While it is possible to chemically alter the composition of liquids to create a beverage resembling wine, this process would not replicate the instantaneous transformation described in the *Bible*. Therefore, the idea of turning water into wine remains a matter of faith rather than scientific fact.

Similarly, the story of Jesus walking on water challenges scientific explanation. According to the laws of physics, it is impossible for a human to walk on water without the aid of some external force, such as a platform or boat. Some have suggested that Jesus may have been walking on a submerged sandbar or a layer of ice, but there is no concrete evidence to support these claims.

From a scientific standpoint, the idea of someone being brought back to life after being clinically dead for a period of time is also highly unlikely. Once the body ceases to function, brain cells begin to die off rapidly, and irreversible damage occurs to major organs. Even with modern medical technology, there is no known method of restoring life to someone who has been dead for a significant amount of time.

Therefore, the idea of someone being raised from the dead remains a matter of faith rather than scientific fact. While some may argue that it is possible that these stories were embellished or misunderstood, the idea of the resurrection of the dead is a central tenet of Christian belief and remains an important part of the religion's history and teachings.

Parting of the Red Sea

The "miracle" of the parting of the Red Sea is a story from the *Old Testament* of the *Bible*. According to the story, the Israelites were fleeing from slavery in Egypt and were pursued by the Egyptian army. They found themselves trapped between the sea and the army, but God intervened by causing the waters of the Red Sea to part, allowing the Israelites to cross safely to the other side. The Egyptians pursued them into the parted sea, but as soon as the Israelites had safely crossed, the waters returned, drowning the entire Egyptian army.

There is no physical evidence that Moses parted the Red Sea as described in the *Bible*. While some scholars believe that the story may be based on historical events, there is no archaeological or geological evidence to support the claim that the Red Sea was ever parted, and many scientists and historians view the story as a myth or legend. In addition, the narrative has been subject to various interpretations and translations over time, leading to debate about the exact location of the crossing and the actual events that may have taken place.

The Ten Plagues of Egypt

The Ten Plagues of Egypt are a series of supernatural events described in the *Book of Exodus*, which are said to have occurred during the enslavement of the Israelites in ancient Egypt. According to the biblical account, Moses, with the help of his brother Aaron, went to the Pharaoh and demanded that he release the Israelites from bondage. When the Pharaoh refused, God sent a series of plagues upon the Egyptians to force them to release the Israelites.

The plagues are described as follows: The Nile River turned to blood, causing the death of fish and making the water undrinkable. The second plague was a swarm of frogs that covered the land. The third plague was a swarm of gnats or lice that infested the people and animals. The fourth plague was a swarm of flies that caused chaos and disease. The fifth plague was the death of livestock, which affected the Egyptian economy. The sixth plague was a skin disease that afflicted people and animals. The seventh plague was a hailstorm that destroyed crops and property. The eighth plague was a swarm of locusts that devoured the remaining crops. The ninth plague was three days of darkness that covered the land. The tenth and final plague was the death of the firstborn son in every Egyptian household, which convinced the Pharaoh to release the Israelites.

The "miraculous" plagues are interpreted as a demonstration of God's power and as punishment for the Egyptians' mistreatment of the Israelites. They are also seen as a way for God to prove his superiority over the Egyptian gods and to establish his authority as the one true God.

The Ten Plagues of Egypt have become a significant part of Jewish and Christian tradition and are often depicted in art and literature. They have also been the subject of scientific and historical inquiry, as scholars have attempted to understand the origins and meanings of these supernatural events.

The Walls of Jericho

The story of the walls of Jericho falling down is recorded in the *Book of Joshua* in the *Old Testament*. According to the story, the Israelites, led by Joshua, had just crossed the Jordan River into the Promised Land and were preparing to take the city of Jericho, which was heavily fortified with walls. God commanded Joshua to have his troops march around the city once a day for six days, and on the seventh day, to march around the city seven times. The priests were to blow trumpets, and then the people were to shout with a great cry. When they did so, the walls of Jericho "miraculously" fell, and the Israelites were able to conquer the city.

This event is seen by many as a miraculous intervention by God in the affairs of humans. The falling of the walls of Jericho is seen as evidence of God's power and as a demonstration of his favor towards the Israelites. It is also viewed as an important event in the history of the Israelites, marking their successful entry into the Promised Land.

However, the story of the walls of Jericho has also been subjected to historical and archaeological scrutiny. Some scholars have questioned the accuracy of the biblical account, arguing that there is no evidence of a city of Jericho being inhabited during the time period when the events were said to have occurred. Others suggest that the walls may have fallen due to an earthquake or other natural disaster, rather than a miraculous intervention.

The Story of Devil's and Swine

The story of devils and swine is a well-known miracle from the *New Testament*, specifically in the *Gospel of Mark*, chapter 5, verses 1-20. The story involves a man possessed by demons who lived among tombs and was uncontrollable. Jesus encounters the man and casts the demons out of him, sending them into a herd of pigs grazing nearby. The pigs then run into the sea and drown, freeing the man from his possession.

This story has been the subject of much discussion and interpretation among theologians and scholars. Some see it as a literal account of an actual event, while others view it as a metaphorical tale meant to convey a deeper message. Regardless of its interpretation, the story is often cited as an example of Jesus' power over evil spirits.

However, the story has also been criticized for its perceived cruelty towards animals. The mass drowning of the pigs has been seen as unnecessary and callous and has led to debates about the ethics of animal treatment in religious contexts.

Furthermore, the story of devils and swine has also been used as a point of contention among skeptics and non-believers. Many argue that the story is implausible and lacks credible or scientific evidence, and that it serves as an example of the absurdity of many religious tales.

Daniel In the Lion's Den

The story of Daniel in the lion's den is a biblical account of a "miracle" in which the prophet Daniel is saved from death after being thrown into a den of lions as punishment for praying to God instead of King Darius. According to the story in the Book of Daniel, Daniel was a high-ranking official in the Babylonian empire who refused to worship the king as a god and continued to pray to his own God, Yahweh. The king, feeling threatened by Daniel's devotion to his own God, issued a decree that anyone caught praying to any god or human being besides the king would be thrown into a den of lions.

Despite the decree, Daniel continued to pray to Yahweh, and he was subsequently caught and thrown into the lion's den. However, God performed a miracle and sent an angel to close the mouths of the lions, preventing them from attacking Daniel. The next morning, when King Darius went to check on Daniel, he was amazed to find him alive and unharmed. He declared Daniel's God to be the true God and ordered that all people in the kingdom should worship him.

Read that again, "ordered that all people in the kingdom should worship him". Interesting story...

In David Hume's essay *Of Miracles*, Hume argues that miracles are a violation of the laws of nature, which are based on experience and observation. He claims that the evidence for miracles is always based on human testimony, which is fallible and subject to error and deception.

Hume argues that, in order to establish a miracle, the testimony would need to be so strong and compelling that it outweighs the evidence against it, including the evidence of the uniformity of nature, which is based on countless experiences of cause and effect. He asserts that it is always more likely that the testimony is mistaken, exaggerated, or fabricated, than that a miracle has actually occurred.

Hume's argument has been influential in the debate over the credibility of miracles, and his skeptical approach to religious claims has been a source of controversy and debate among philosophers and theologians.

Hume's views on religion were highly controversial for his time. He was critical of traditional religious beliefs and argued that there was no rational basis for belief in miracles or the existence of God. He famously wrote, "A wise man proportions his belief to the evidence" and argued that miracles were violations of the laws of nature and therefore could not be accepted on the basis of testimony alone.

The French curate Meslier was a controversial figure in his time, known for his rejection of the miracles described in the *New Testament*. Meslier believed that these stories were invented by priests in order to maintain their power over the masses, and that they were harmful to the idea of a benevolent God. Among these were stories such as the devil carrying Jesus to the top of a mountain, the marriage of Cana, and the story of the loaves and fishes. He saw the miracles as ridiculous tales that were injurious to the goodness of the Supreme Being.

Meslier's rejection of miracles was part of a larger critique of the Catholic Church, which he believed was corrupt and self-serving. He saw the Church as an institution that used religion to control and manipulate people, rather than as an organization dedicated to promoting the values of truth and morality. For Meslier, the pursuit of truth and morality was a better basis for religion than blind obedience to religious leaders.

Meslier's ideas were considered radical in his time, and he was posthumously recognized as an important figure in the history of French atheism. His rejection of miracles and his criticism of the Catholic Church helped to pave the way for the Enlightenment, which emphasized reason and scientific inquiry over superstition and dogma. Meslier's legacy can still be seen in the modern secular movements that prioritize critical thinking and rationality in the face of religious dogma.

The belief in miracles has been linked to the dangerous practice of accusing people of witchcraft, which was prevalent during the darker ages when the Church held more power. Sadly, many innocent people were prosecuted and executed as a result of these accusations, and the clergy were often the chief promoters of these baseless charges. This highlights the danger of blindly accepting supernatural beliefs without evidence or critical examination, as it can lead to unjust and even deadly consequences.

The ancient philosophers recognized the perils of superstition and ranked it among the vices. They saw it as a terrible evil that arises from education or the natural weakness of the human mind, oppressing nearly the whole of mankind. This view is still relevant today, as many people continue to be manipulated by superstitious beliefs and false claims of miraculous events.

In many schools of divinity, young people are taught to believe in a specific manner that suits the theologian, rather than being encouraged to think critically and form their own beliefs based on evidence and reason. However, unbiased reflection is crucial for discovering what is true and avoiding the pitfalls of superstition and blind faith. Ultimately, the pursuit of knowledge and critical thinking is essential for overcoming the dangers of supernatural beliefs and promoting a more rational and enlightened society.

In my opinion, the requirement to believe in miracles goes against the principles of free will and authenticity. It is disingenuous to impose supernatural beliefs on others, especially if such beliefs lack any empirical evidence. The absence of modern-day miracles leads one to question the veracity of religious dogma and its claims of divine intervention.

The lack of miraculous events in modern times suggests that the concept of miracles was created as a means of consolidating power and control over the masses. Religion has often been used to manipulate people's beliefs and actions, and the idea of miracles can serve as a tool for this purpose. The educated segment of society is still susceptible to the influence of religious leaders, but the proliferation of knowledge and access to information has made it harder to maintain such beliefs.

Miracles are not consistent with the laws of nature, the principles of reason, and the human experience. Instead, it seems more plausible that people in the past may have simply spread false claims rather than actual miracles taking place. I find the concept of a supreme power violating the unchanging laws of nature just for the benefit of a few humans to be a ridiculous and disrespectful idea.

In my opinion, religions that do not rely on rational and natural explanations are often based on superstitions, deceptions, and lies. The use of miracles has been a widespread strategy used by various religious groups to attain influence and authority. Unfortunately, these tactics have been primarily aimed at manipulating the uninformed and unsuspecting masses.

I believe that the widespread dissemination of books about theological mysteries and miracles (ie: religious texts) has caused great harm and suffering for humanity. These types of books have led to intolerance, religious wars, and terrible devastation throughout history. In my opinion, the only way to improve our understanding of the world is through the use of reason. I don't think that any book can improve our reasoning abilities unless it provides convincing evidence to support its claims.

The idea of miracles goes against both reason and experience. In the past, various nations have come up with unbelievable stories of supposed miracles, and the most ridiculous ones were usually created in places where the majority of people were uneducated and vulnerable to manipulation by their religious leaders.

In my view, a revelation that does not allow for examination and judgment based on reason is not helpful and actually inhibits the use of reason. I believe that it's important to critically examine religious texts and teachings to determine their validity and relevance in our lives. The use of miracles as a means of gaining power and influence is a common tactic among religious groups, and I believe it's important to be aware of this in order to avoid being manipulated.

Every revealed religion has had its code of miracles, and each religion's priests have denied the truth of all others, claiming that their own doctrine is the only infallible one. Belief in faith alone is based on obligation, whereas knowledge is based on reason and common sense. Faith is the best working tool of every priest, and without it, they cannot secure a blind obedience.

Ultimately, I believe that reason is the only way to improve our understanding of the world and to prevent the kind of harm and suffering that has been caused by religious conflicts throughout history. While I acknowledge the value of faith and spirituality, I believe that it's important to approach these topics with a critical and rational mindset in order to make informed decisions about our beliefs and actions.

The order of nature is something truly remarkable and awe-inspiring. The fact that hundreds of millions of globes revolve around millions of suns in perfect harmony is, in itself, what I would call "a miracle". However, this order is not the result of supernatural intervention, but rather the operation of immutable and inviolable laws of nature.

Therefore, I suggest that the idea of a miracle is a concept misunderstood. Rather than attributing events to the supernatural or divine, I believe that we should strive to understand the natural laws that govern the universe. Through scientific inquiry and rational exploration, we can gain a deeper understanding of the workings of the natural world and appreciate the complexity and beauty of the universe in which we live.

While some may argue that this approach lacks the sense of awe and wonder that comes with belief in miracles, I believe that the opposite is true. Understanding the natural laws that govern the universe can give us a greater appreciation for the sheer magnitude and complexity of the world around us. It can also inspire us to continue to explore and discover the mysteries of the universe, and to seek out the answers to the questions that have fascinated humanity for centuries.

The Devil and the Church

As I see it, the Church's relationship with the devil is complex and symbiotic. The Church and the devil seem to benefit from each other's existence. The Church's claim to weaken or destroy the devil's power seems to be a mere folly because the Church's own interests are promoted by increasing the devil's power.

This raises serious questions about the Church's true intentions and motivations. Does the Church really want to eradicate evil, or does it need evil to maintain its own power and influence? It's a troubling thought, but one that must be considered.

The Church's dependence on the devil raises concerns about the authenticity of its teachings. If the devil is necessary for the Church's existence, it begs the question of whether the Church's teachings are truly in the best interest of its followers or if they serve to maintain the Church's own power and influence.

The Church's views on science have often been at odds with modern scientific discoveries and advancements. This has led to conflicts between religion and science, which can have negative consequences for society. It's important for the Church to recognize the importance of scientific progress and to embrace new ideas and knowledge, rather than clinging to outdated beliefs that may hinder progress.

In today's world, where science and technology are advancing at an unprecedented rate, it's essential that the Church is willing to adapt and evolve its teachings to keep up with the times. Only by doing so can the Church continue to play a positive role in the lives of its followers and in society as a whole.

We cannot rely on mystery, miracle, and obscurity to lead us to knowledge or virtue. These concepts are often used to promote imposture and ignorance and suppress reason and natural understanding. In fact, goodness, virtue, and knowledge are unlikely to be found in such contexts.

Religion, while important to many, is not a natural phenomenon. It is an artificial construct that relies on delusive inventions and pretended mysteries and inspirations of impostors. Inspiration, which can be manipulated and distorted by those who claim to possess it, has given birth to saintly villainy, religious lies, and false miracles that are pernicious to human beings and scandalous to the idea of an omnipotent power.

Every hypothesis that is not founded in nature is absurd and cannot be the object of rational belief. Nature is consistent and reliable, and the only true religion can be based on its laws and principles. The laws of omnipotence cannot contradict or be less evident than those of nature, and therefore, we should not blindly follow the authority of priests without examining it with reason.

Fear and Superstition

The Church's promotion of religious dogma and its restriction of scientific inquiry is concerning. It seems that the Church benefits from instilling fear and superstition in people to maintain its power over them. This is troubling because it raises questions about the Church's true intentions and motivations. Are they really trying to eradicate evil or are they perpetuating it for their own gain?

Moreover, the argument that priests and religion strengthen the power of the devil is a thought-provoking one. It's unsettling to think that the Church's claim to weaken the devil's power may actually be promoting it. However, the claim that if the maxims of the Christian religion respecting science were universally followed, no political society could exist is not entirely clear and lacks sufficient evidence.

One of the most concerning examples of the Church's manipulation of fear and superstition is the role it played in the accusations of witchcraft, which resulted in the murder of many innocent people. The greatest philosophers of antiquity believed that superstition was a vice and that true happiness and virtue came from practicing reason and morality.

The connection between the belief in miracles and superstition lies in the fact that both rely on a suspension of natural laws and empirical evidence. Superstition often involves a belief in supernatural entities or events that are not supported by reason or evidence. Similarly, belief in miracles often involves a belief in divine intervention or supernatural powers that cannot be explained by natural laws or empirical evidence.

Ancient philosophers such as Aristotle and Cicero believed that superstition was a terrible evil that oppressed humanity. They argued that it was born out of ignorance and fear, and that it led people to make irrational decisions and engage in harmful practices. They believed that the only way to combat superstition was through reason and education.

Similarly, the belief in miracles can lead to irrational decision-making and harmful practices, particularly when it is used to justify violence or discrimination against those who do not share the same beliefs. It can also be used to manipulate and control the masses by those in positions of power.

As far as we know, there is no concrete evidence to support the claim that an all-powerful being interferes with the natural world through miracles or other supernatural occurrences. While some people may believe in the existence of such a force, there is no conclusive proof to support these beliefs. Instead, many explanations for the workings of the natural world can be found through scientific investigation and observation.

It is possible that some people find comfort in the idea of a higher power that intervenes in the world, providing hope and reassurance in the face of life's difficulties. However, it is important to distinguish between faith and evidence-based claims. Without reliable evidence to support the occurrence of miracles, it is reasonable to approach such claims with skepticism and to focus instead on rational and empirical explanations for the workings of the natural world.

Anyone who uses logic and common sense would agree that the Church's promotion of fear and superstition and its restriction of scientific inquiry raise questions about its true intentions and motivations. We must embrace the power of reason and the light of nature to gain a deeper understanding of ourselves and the world around us. By doing so, we can break free from the shackles of superstition and deception and pursue knowledge and virtue in a more honest and authentic way.

The Pursuit of Truth

The pursuit of truth and morality should be at the forefront of any religious practice. Blindly following religious leaders and accepting their teachings without questioning or critical analysis can lead to dangerous and harmful beliefs. It is important to question authority and seek out evidence to support religious claims. This is especially true in today's world where access to information and the ability to critically analyze information is more accessible than ever before.

Religious leaders are not infallible and can be (and usually are) influenced by their own biases and agendas. The pursuit of truth and morality requires an open mind and a willingness to challenge established beliefs and traditions. This process can be uncomfortable and unsettling for some, but it is necessary for growth and progress. Blind obedience to religious leaders can stifle this process and lead to a stagnant and dogmatic religious practice.

Furthermore, a religious practice based on truth and morality is more inclusive and respectful of diverse beliefs and perspectives. Blind obedience to religious leaders often leads to a narrow and exclusive interpretation of religious teachings, which can lead to intolerance and conflict. By prioritizing truth and morality, religious practitioners can create a more welcoming and accepting community that values diversity and promotes understanding.

The pursuit of truth and morality is essential for a healthy and progressive religious practice. Blind obedience to religious leaders can lead to harmful beliefs and practices, and can stifle growth and progress. By questioning authority, seeking evidence, and prioritizing truth and morality, religious practitioners can create a more inclusive, diverse, and respectful com In today's world, correcting centuries-old religious abuses and removing deeply ingrained prejudices is a daunting task. Private interests, pride, passion, and obstinacy often stand in the way of progress. One of the main challenges of reforming religion is that people are often resistant to change and view any attempt to correct them as an attack on their judgment and intelligence.

In the past, when ignorance was more widespread, people believed that the almighty power revealed his anger through miracles and other supernatural events. However, in modern times, we understand that such phenomena are simply common effects of natural causes. Despite this understanding, many still hold on to the belief that they are the chosen ones, favored by a divine being who resembles them in every way.

This highlights the danger of creating a God in our own image, as it perpetuates prejudices and reinforces existing power structures. It is important for us to challenge our own beliefs and biases in order to create a more just and equitable society. We must be willing to question established dogmas and seek the truth, even if it means confronting uncomfortable realities. Ultimately, the pursuit of knowledge and the rejection of superstition and prejudice is essential for a society to progress and thrive.

In today's world, correcting centuries-old religious abuses and removing deeply ingrained prejudices is a daunting task. Private interests, pride, passion, and obstinacy often stand in the way of progress. One of the main challenges of reforming religion is that people are often resistant to change and view any attempt to correct them as an attack on their judgment and intelligence.

In the past, when ignorance was more widespread, people believed that the almighty power revealed his anger through miracles and other supernatural events. However, in modern times, we understand that such phenomena are simply common effects of natural causes. Despite this understanding, many still hold on to the belief that they are the chosen ones, favored by a divine being who resembles them in every way.

This highlights the danger of creating a God in our own image, as it perpetuates prejudices and reinforces existing power structures. It is important for us to challenge our own beliefs and biases in order to create a more just and equitable society. We must be willing to question established dogmas and seek the truth, even if it means confronting uncomfortable realities. Ultimately, the pursuit of knowledge and the rejection of superstition and prejudice is essential for a society to progress and thrive.

To achieve true happiness and eliminate the sources of misery in our lives, it is essential to free our minds from the obstructions that hold us back and to focus on the study of the physical and intellectual powers displayed in nature. The pursuit of imaginary beings and their supposed supernatural actions, on the other hand, is a futile and misguided endeavor that can never yield useful knowledge.

By engaging in scientific inquiry and analysis, we can gain a deeper understanding of the natural world and the laws that govern it. Through observation and experimentation, we can uncover new truths about the behavior of living organisms, the workings of the human mind, and the properties of matter and energy. These discoveries can lead to technological advancements that improve our lives and allow us to explore the world around us in new and exciting ways.

Moreover, studying the physical and intellectual powers displayed in nature can help us develop a greater appreciation for the natural world and its many wonders. By understanding the intricacies of the natural world, we can gain a deeper respect for the forces that shape our lives and the lives of all living beings. In this way, the pursuit of scientific knowledge can lead to a greater sense of connection with the world around us and a deeper understanding of our place within it.

Jesus Christ

The founder of Christianity, Jesus Christ, is regarded as one of the most influential figures in history. He lived in the Roman Empire during a time of political and social upheaval, and his teachings and actions were seen as a challenge to the established authorities of the day. Jesus was a moral and spiritual leader who sought to reform the religious practices of his time and promote a message of love, forgiveness, and compassion.

Jesus' teachings and actions were often controversial and challenged the status quo. He spoke out against religious leaders who he believed were corrupt and hypocritical, and he attracted a following of people who were drawn to his message of hope and salvation. Jesus' teachings emphasized the importance of love and compassion for all people, regardless of their social status or background.

While Jesus himself did not explicitly claim to have supernatural powers, the religion that bears his name has been associated with miracles and other supernatural events. This is largely due to the way in which the religion developed over time, as his teachings were interpreted and embellished by his followers. The concept of miracles is often seen as a way to validate the teachings of Jesus and reinforce the idea that he was a divine figure.

Despite the controversies and debates surrounding the nature of Jesus and his teachings, his influence has endured for centuries. Christianity has become one of the world's largest religions, with millions of followers across the globe.

God's Decrees of the Order of Nature

According to my understanding, nothing rational and consistent can be learned from what is often referred to as the "commands of God." The so-called decrees of God are nothing more than the universal laws of nature or eternal verity and necessity. The more we learn about the workings of the natural world, the more we come to understand the supreme power that governs it. By understanding the natural causes and effects of things, we can gain a deeper appreciation of the immutable essence of that power.

Jesus Christ, who was a reformer and moralist, likely did not possess any supernatural powers. However, as the religion developed a priesthood, miracles were attributed to him to further the interests of the clergy and to appease the fears of the superstitious masses. Despite appearing as manifest and self-evident impostures to some, miracles have persisted through many ages and nations due to the zealous exertions and overwhelming influence of the privileged body of men.

The Christian virtue of faith, which is often held up as the highest of virtues, requires a complete abandonment of reason, an unwavering belief in improbable events and doctrines, and an uncritical submission to the authority of priests. This kind of faith has been the root of much madness, hatred, persecution, and destruction throughout history, as it degrades and debases the truth.

To safeguard our natural right to think, write, and judge for ourselves in matters of religion is crucial to avoid the manipulation of a tyrannical and self-serving clergy. It is only by preserving this right that we can liberate ourselves from the confines of blind faith and superstition and embrace the pursuit of truth and knowledge with unwavering conviction and bravery.

As we move forward, it is crucial that we work towards restoring the world to its primitive religion of nature, which was the intended purpose of the law and the prophets. The reformation that Jesus envisioned was the establishment of this pure and simple religion among his people, many of whom were eager to embrace it. Jesus' message was of love, kindness, and compassion and it has been replaced by a dogmatic and often oppressive system of beliefs. The church deviated from this doctrine and instead perverted it to suit their own corrupt interests, leading to the rise of a destructive hireling priesthood that has caused great harm to society, and continues to do so. So much for Jesus' teachings.

And what about people who have always looked to the natural world as a symbol of something greater or divine?

The Spaniards' treatment of the indigenous people of America was nothing short of a brutal and systematic campaign of extermination, motivated by greed, power, and a sense of racial and cultural superiority.

Rather than seeking to understand and learn from the rich and diverse cultures of the Americas, the Spaniards saw the native people as savages to be conquered and exploited. They used their religious beliefs as a tool of oppression, forcing conversion to Christianity upon the native population and using violence and coercion to suppress any resistance.

The idea that God would sanction such violence and oppression is not only morally repugnant but also contradicts the very essence of Christianity, which teaches love, compassion, and respect for all people, regardless of their race or culture. It is a perversion of the true message of the Bible, which promotes justice, mercy, and humility.

Furthermore, it is essential to recognize the role that cultural imperialism and racism played in the conquest of the Americas. The belief that European culture and religion were superior to those of the native people was a driving force behind the Spaniards' actions, and this mindset continues to have devastating effects on indigenous peoples around the world.

As responsible and ethical individuals, it is our duty to critically examine and challenge the actions of those in power, including religious and political authorities. We must reject any notion that justifies violence, discrimination, or oppression in the name of religion or any other belief system.

It is therefore imperative that we abolish this harmful priesthood, as their contentions and animosities have caused much strife and division within families and have even led to wars that have plagued nations for centuries. We must strive towards a more unified and harmonious society, one that is not plagued by the artificial constructs of organized religion. By embracing the principles of primitive simplicity, we can work towards a brighter future that is grounded in truth, reason, and compassion for all.

Chapter Four: The Retelling

The Torah

The *Pentateuch* and the *Torah* refer to the same set of five books of the *Hebrew Bible*: Genesis, Exodus, Leviticus, Numbers, and Deuteronomy. The term Pentateuch is derived from the Greek word pentateuchos, meaning "five scrolls," while the term Torah comes from the Hebrew word torah, which means "instruction" or "teaching."

The *Torah/Pentateuch* is considered to be the foundational text of Judaism and contains many important stories and laws that continue to shape Jewish religious and cultural practices today.

These books form the central text of Judaism and contains the foundational narratives and laws of the Jewish faith. The *Torah/Pentateuch* is also recognized as a sacred text by Christians and Muslims. It is believed to have been written by Moses, though some scholars suggest that it was written by multiple authors over a long period of time.

Stories within the *Torah/Pentateuch* contain numerous miraculous stories that have captivated believers and skeptics alike for centuries. However, some scholars suggest that many of these stories were not original to the Jewish people but rather were borrowed from the traditions of other Pagan nations.

It's important to note that the Jews had been in slavery and captivity amongst other nations before, and it's likely that they borrowed and adapted stories from these cultures during their time of captivity. Additionally, it was common practice for ancient cultures to adopt and adapt the stories and beliefs of other cultures, often incorporating them into their own religious traditions.

The *Torah/Pentateuch* contains multiple references to the worship of other gods and goddesses, suggesting that the early Jewish people may have incorporated elements of Paganism into their own religious beliefs.

While the exact origins of the miraculous stories found in the *Torah/Pentateuch* may be uncertain, what is clear is that many of these stories have become foundational to the beliefs and practices of Judaism, Christianity, and Islam. Many of the stories found in the *Torah/Pentateuch*, have parallels in the myths and legends of other ancient cultures.

Noah's Ark

The Babylonian *Epic of Gilgamesh* is an ancient text that recounts the adventures of Gilgamesh, a legendary king of Uruk. The epic is believed to have been written between 2150-1400 BCE and contains many elements that are similar to stories found in the *Hebrew Bible*, including a flood narrative. In the story, the gods decide to send a flood to destroy all living creatures on Earth, but a man named Utnapishtim is warned of the impending disaster and builds a large boat to save himself, his family, and a variety of animals.

The story of Noah's Ark in the *Hebrew Bible* shares many similarities with the Babylonian flood narrative. In both stories, a man is warned of an impending flood and builds a boat to save himself, his family, and animals. The flood is sent by a higher power to destroy all living creatures on Earth, but the man and his family are able to survive by building the boat and riding out the storm.

The Sumerian myth of Ziusudra, also known as the *Epic of Ziusudra*, tells the story of a king who is warned by the god Enki of an impending flood that will destroy all of humanity. Enki instructs Ziusudra to build a massive boat, and to bring along with him his family, animals, and skilled craftsmen.

Ziusudra follows Enki's instructions and survives the flood, eventually landing his boat on the summit of a mountain. He then offers a sacrifice to the gods, and is granted immortality by An, the god of heaven.

The similarities between the three stories have led many scholars to believe that the biblical account of Noah's Ark may have been influenced by earlier flood myths, such as the one found in the *Epic of Gilgamesh*.

The story of Ziusudra is often seen as a precursor to the biblical story of Noah's Ark, as it shares many similarities, including the warning of a flood, the construction of a boat, and the survival of a chosen few.

This theory is supported by the fact that the *Hebrew Bible* was written during a time when the Israelites were in contact with other cultures and would have been exposed to their myths and legends. Additionally, the Babylonian empire was known to have conquered the region where the Israelites lived, which would have provided ample opportunity for cultural exchange.

One God

The concept of a unified Supreme Being was not present in early Judaism, and the idea appears to have been borrowed from other ancient religions. One such religion was the Egyptian religion of Isis, which featured a belief in a single, all-powerful deity.

The concept of a unified Supreme Being refers to the idea that there is only one God or deity who is the ultimate creator and ruler of the universe. This belief is common in many monotheistic religions, such as Judaism, Christianity, and Islam. The concept of a unified Supreme Being suggests that all aspects of the universe are part of a single, integrated whole that is governed by a single divine will or plan. This belief is often associated with the idea of divine providence, which suggests that everything that happens in the world is part of a larger plan or purpose that is guided by the Supreme Being.

It is believed that Moses, who was born in Egypt was likely influenced by this belief and incorporated it into his own teachings.

This theory is further supported by the fact that many of the symbols and rituals used in Judaism bear a striking resemblance to those used in the Egyptian religion. For example, the use of the menorah in the Jewish Temple is similar to the use of the ankh in the Egyptian Temple, and the practice of circumcision, which is an important part of Jewish tradition, was also practiced by the Egyptians.

These similarities may suggest that there was cultural exchange and influence between the two civilizations, or that some practices were simply common to the wider region and adopted by different groups.

It is also worth noting that the Jewish religion underwent significant changes and revisions throughout its history, and the concept of a single, all-powerful deity did not become fully integrated into Jewish theology until after the Babylonian exile. Therefore, it is entirely plausible that Moses, drawing upon his knowledge of Egyptian religion and his own spiritual experiences, played a key role in the development of this idea within Judaism.

The Story of Creation

The story of the creation of the world in six days is an example of how religious beliefs and ideas have been influenced and borrowed from other cultures throughout history. The similarities between the creation stories found in the *Bible* and those in the mythologies of various eastern nations suggest that the Hebrews were not operating in isolation but were instead part of a wider cultural and religious milieu.

The Babylonians, for example, had their own creation story known as the *Enuma Elish*, which tells of a series of divine battles that culminate in the creation of the world. In this myth, the world is created through a violent struggle between the gods Tiamat and Marduk.

The Sumerians had a creation myth known as the *Eridu Genesis*, which describes the creation of the world as a series of events that unfolded over several stages.

The the ancient Egyptian creation story describes the creation of the world by the god Atum, who emerges from the primordial waters and creates the world through his own power.

The Hindu creation story, found in the *Rigveda*, describes the creation of the world through the sacrifice of the primeval being, Purusha.

Interestingly, they all predate the *Bible*. Despite the differences in the details of these creation myths, they all share the common theme of a divine being or beings creating world over a period of time.

This suggests that the idea of a supreme creator or god was a common belief among ancient cultures, and that the Hebrews were not unique in their understanding of the divine.

Therefore, it is reasonable to conclude that the story of creation in the *Bible* was influenced by these earlier sources, and that the Hebrews borrowed and adapted these stories to suit their own religious beliefs and practices.

Adam and Eve

In Greek mythology, Prometheus and Epimetheus were brothers and Titans who played important roles in the creation of mankind. According to the myth, Prometheus created humans out of clay, while Epimetheus was in charge of giving them qualities such as speed, strength, and agility. However, he ended up giving away all of the positive traits to animals, leaving humans vulnerable and defenseless.

The story of Adam and Eve in the *Bible* shares some similarities with the story of Prometheus and Epimetheus. In the *Bible*, God creates Adam out of dust and breathes life into him, and then creates Eve from one of Adam's ribs. Like Epimetheus, God gives Adam and Eve free will and the ability to make choices, which leads to their eventual downfall when they eat from the forbidden tree.

Gayomart is a figure in Persian mythology who is considered to be the first human. According to the myth, Gayomart was created by Ahura Mazda, the god of creation and wisdom, and lived a peaceful life in a garden paradise. However, he was eventually killed by the evil spirit Ahriman, and his body was used to create the various parts of the world, such as the sky and the stars. Gayomart is seen as a symbol of purity and goodness in Persian culture and is often depicted in art as a beautiful, radiant figure.

Mashya and Mashyana are also figures in Persian mythology and are considered to be the first man and woman. According to the myth, they were created by the god Ahura Mazda from the semen and the egg of the primeval bull. They lived in a paradise-like garden and were the parents of the first human couple. Like Gayomart, they are seen as symbols of purity and goodness in Persian culture and are often depicted in art as beautiful, radiant figures.

In the story of Enki and Ninhursag from Sumerian mythology, Enki creates humans and gives them free will. However, the humans become too noisy and start to annoy the gods. As a result, the gods punish the humans, causing Enki to become sad and worried about their well-being. Enki then creates a goddess named Ninhursag to help him heal the humans. Together, they create a new type of human that is more respectful and obedient to the gods. This story deals with the consequences of misusing free will and the need for guidance and correction.

In the story of Coyote from Native American mythology, Coyote creates humans and gives them free will. However, the humans become greedy and selfish, causing conflict and destruction. Coyote realizes that he must intervene to prevent the humans from destroying themselves. He teaches them important lessons about the importance of cooperation and selflessness, and he helps them to overcome their selfish tendencies. This story deals with the consequences of misusing free will and the need for wisdom and guidance in using it wisely.

While the stories of Adam and Eve and others are not identical, the parallels between them are striking. All the stories deal with the creation of mankind, the gift of free will, and the consequences of making bad choices.

Crossing the Red Sea

The story of the Israelites crossing the Red Sea is a well-known and celebrated event in the Bible. According to the story, the Israelites, who were enslaved in Egypt, were led out of captivity by Moses and miraculously crossed the Red Sea, with the waters parting to allow them to pass and then closing in on the pursuing Egyptian army.

Interestingly, there are similarities between this story and the journey of the Greek god Bacchus. According to Greek mythology, Bacchus, also known as Dionysus, was a god of wine and fertility who traveled with his followers to spread his teachings and liberate people from their everyday worries. In one version of his story, he leads his followers across a river, with the waters parting to allow them to cross.

While the details of the two stories are different, the idea of crossing a body of water and being delivered from danger or oppression is a common motif in many cultures and mythologies. It is possible that the story of the Israelites crossing the Red Sea was influenced by earlier stories and traditions, including the story of Bacchus.

This highlights the fact that many religious and mythological stories share common themes and motifs, and that the stories we know today may have been influenced by earlier traditions and cultures.

The Story of Joseph

The story of Joseph, which is found in the book of Genesis, tells the tale of Joseph, the son of Jacob, who is sold into slavery by his jealous brothers. He is then taken to Egypt, where he rises to prominence as an advisor to the Pharaoh. The story has many similarities to the story of Yusuf in the Quran and the story of Yuya in the Ancient Egyptian texts. However, it is also believed to have been borrowed from an Arabian story called "The Story of Yusuf and Zulaikha," which shares many similarities with the biblical account.

In the Arabian story, Yusuf is also the son of a prophet and is sold into slavery by his brothers. He is then taken to Egypt, where he becomes the chief steward of a wealthy woman named Zulaikha. Like Joseph in the Bible, he is eventually thrown into prison after being falsely accused of a crime. The story has many of the same themes as the biblical story, including jealousy, betrayal, and redemption. Many scholars believe that the story of Joseph in the Bible was heavily influenced by this earlier Arabian tale, with some even suggesting that the biblical account is a direct translation of the Arabian original.

The Miracle of Manna

In the *Bible*, the Israelites, after fleeing from slavery in Egypt, become hungry and are sustained in the wilderness by a miraculous food called manna which God provides for them. It is described as a sweet bread-like substance that falls from the sky every morning. The miracle of the manna is not unique to the Bible and can be found in other cultures as well. For example, there are accounts of a similar substance in Arabian folklore, where it is known as "samgh" or "saint's bread."

According to some scholars, the substance known as samgh was actually a type of plant that grew in the Arabian Peninsula and was used as a source of food by nomadic tribes. This plant, which is known as alhagi maurorum, is still found in the region today and is believed to have been the basis for the story of the manna in the *Bible*.

Similarly, there also accounts of a similar substance in Sicilian folklore, where it is known as "manna." In this case, the substance was believed to be a sap that was secreted by the ash tree and was used as a sweetener and medicine.

The story of the manna in the *Bible* is not necessarily a miraculous event, but rather a reflection of the natural world and the way in which ancient peoples sought to understand and explain it through mythology and folklore.

These stories demonstrate the universal human experience of hunger and the need for sustenance, as well as the human desire for divine intervention or assistance in times of need.

The Brazen Serpent

In the biblical story, Moses and the Israelites are wandering in the wilderness and are being plagued by fiery serpents. In order to cure them, God instructs Moses to make a bronze serpent and put it on a pole, and whoever looks at it will be healed.

Some scholars have suggested that this story is likely an invention of the Egyptian priests, as they were known to have used a similar symbol of a serpent on a pole as a healing charm. The symbol was known as the uraeus and was associated with the goddess Wadjet. The Egyptians believed that the serpent represented healing and protection, and it was often worn as a protective amulet.

It is possible that Moses, who was raised as an Egyptian prince and would have been familiar with Egyptian religious practices, incorporated this symbol into his own religion. The story of the Brazen Serpent may have been a way to explain the use of the symbol to the Israelites and to give it a new meaning within their own religious context.

However, it is also possible that the story is entirely fictional and was created as a way to illustrate the power of faith and obedience to God. Regardless of its origins, the story has remained a significant part of Jewish and Christian tradition.

Pillars of Smoke and Fire

The "pillar of fire" and "pillar of smoke" are mentioned in the *Bible* as miraculous signs that guided the Israelites during their journey through the wilderness. However, some scholars argue that these were not actually supernatural occurrences, but rather common military usages that were later turned into miracles by the Jewish compilers.

In ancient times, armies would often use columns of smoke or fire to signal their movements and communicate with one another. A pillar of smoke during the day or a pillar of fire at night would be easily visible from a distance and could be used to coordinate troop movements or communicate important information.

The idea of a pillar of fire or smoke as a symbol of divine presence was not unique to the Israelites. It was a common symbol in many ancient Near Eastern religions, including those of the Egyptians and Babylonians. It is possible that the Israelites borrowed this symbol from their neighbors and incorporated it into their own religious practices.

Throughout history, there have been numerous instances where military tactics or events were transformed into divine intervention in religious texts. For example, in the Bible, the story of the Battle of Jericho describes how the walls of the city were brought down by the blast of a trumpet. While this may seem like a miraculous event, some scholars argue that it could have been the result of military tactics, such as a well-timed attack on the walls or the use of siege engines.

Similarly, in Hindu mythology, the story of the Battle of Kurukshetra in the epic Mahabharata includes numerous instances of divine intervention, such as the use of celestial weapons and the intervention of gods and demigods. However, some scholars argue that these elements were added later to the story to glorify the warrior caste and justify their use of violence in war.

In both cases, military tactics or events were transformed into divine intervention in order to lend greater significance and meaning to the events. It is likely that similar transformations occurred in other religious texts throughout history, as people sought to make sense of the events around them and find meaning in the chaos of war and conflict.

It is also possible that the Israelites used this same military tactic during their journey through the wilderness, and that the writers of the *Bible* later exaggerated these signals into miraculous events.

Sacrificing the Daughter

In the *Old Testament*, Jephtha is a judge of Israel who makes a vow to God, promising that if he is victorious in battle, he will sacrifice the first thing that comes out of his house upon his return. Tragically, it is his daughter who comes out to greet him, and he ultimately sacrifices her to fulfill his vow.

Similarly, in Greek mythology, Agamemnon is a king who sacrifices his daughter Iphigenia in order to appease the goddess Artemis and ensure a successful voyage to Troy during the Trojan War. The story has many parallels to that of Jephtha, including the idea of a father sacrificing his daughter for the sake of a vow or divine intervention.

It is possible that the story of Jephtha sacrificing his daughter was influenced by the Greek tradition of Agamemnon and Iphigenia, as the Israelites would have been exposed to Greek culture through their interactions with neighboring nations. Additionally, the two stories share common themes and motifs that suggest a cultural influence.

Samson and the Lion

The story of Samson in the *Book of Judges* tells of a man with superhuman strength who performs heroic feats such as slaying a lion with his bare hands and destroying an entire temple by pushing down its pillars. These exploits bear striking similarities to those of the Greek hero Hercules, who also possesses great strength and performs incredible feats such as slaying the Nemean lion and completing the Twelve Labors assigned to him by the gods.

In addition, the story of Samson shares similarities with that of the Phoenician hero Melqart, who is also known for his great strength and heroic deeds. Both Samson and Melqart are associated with pillars, with Samson pushing down the pillars of the temple and Melqart being symbolized by two pillars at the temple of Tyre.

These similarities suggest that the story of Samson was influenced by both Greek and Phoenician mythology, with the Israelites borrowing elements from these cultures to create their own heroic figure.

Many of the miraculous and fantastic stories in the *Torah/Pentateuch* have striking similarities to stories from other ancient cultures and traditions. This has led many scholars to question the authenticity and originality of these stories and suggest that they were likely borrowed or adapted from other sources.

These similarities also raise the question of whether the stories in the *Torah/Pentateuch* are truly evidence of divine intervention, or if they were simply borrowed and adapted from other sources. Some scholars argue that the stories were likely used to explain natural phenomena, historical events, or to promote certain religious beliefs or practices.

Therefore, while these stories may hold important cultural and religious significance, they should not necessarily be taken at face value as proof of divine intervention. Rather, they should be studied and analyzed in the context of their cultural and historical origins to gain a better understanding of their significance and meaning.

Similarities and affinities can be found in many religions, including the presence of miracles, oracles, and predictions. In addition, it is common for heathen gods to be dethroned and replaced by others in various religious traditions.

It appears that many of the miraculous stories in the *Torah/Pentateuch* were not original but rather based on earlier myths and legends from various cultures. This suggests that the Jewish writers may have borrowed from these cultures to create their own stories. Moreover, the hyperbolic and exaggerated nature of these stories raises questions about their authenticity and originality.

Hyperbole

I've already shared how the story of Noah's flood in the *Bible* is believed to have been influenced by earlier flood myths from Egypt and Greece. However, the Jewish version exaggerates the extent of the flood by claiming that it covered the entire earth, despite the fact that the existence of the American continent was unknown to them.

The Tower of Babel

The story of the Tower of Babel in the Bible is likely a borrowed tale from the ancient Tower of Belus in Babylon, a famous temple and observatory built by the Chaldeans. The tower was said to be built to reach the heavens and was described by Herodotus as a massive square structure with sides measuring two furlongs and equal height and width. The story tells of the confusion of languages and the dispersal of the Chaldeans.

The ancient Tower of Belus in Babylon is believed to have been built in the 6th century BCE, while the story of the Tower of Babel is believed to have been written in the 5th century BCE. Therefore, the Tower of Belus was constructed before the story of the Tower of Babel was written down.

The two stories share some similarities, including the idea of a tower reaching up to the heavens and a belief in the power of human beings to build structures that can rival the divine. However, the stories also have significant differences, such as the motivation behind the construction of the tower and the consequences of its construction.

The Talking Serpent

The story of Adam and Eve in the Bible describes the creation of the first humans, who were placed in the Garden of Eden and given the task of tending to it. However, they were forbidden from eating from the Tree of Knowledge of Good and Evil. The serpent, who is depicted as the devil, tempts Eve into eating from the tree, telling her that she will gain knowledge and become like God. Eve eats from the tree and convinces Adam to do the same, leading to their expulsion from the Garden of Eden.

The Egyptian fable of the Agathodaemon tells a similar story, with the first woman being tempted by a talking serpent to eat from a forbidden tree.

However, in this fable, the serpent is not portrayed as evil, but rather as a good genius or a benefactor who helps the woman to achieve enlightenment and become more godlike. The story celebrates the serpent as a symbol of wisdom and knowledge, rather than as a symbol of evil.

The differences between these two stories illustrate the cultural and religious perspectives of the societies in which they were created. In the Hebrew tradition, the serpent was already associated with evil and temptation, and so it was a natural choice to make the serpent the tempter in the story of Adam and Eve. The negative portrayal of the serpent reinforced the idea of sin and temptation as being harmful to human beings.

On the other hand, in the Egyptian tradition, the serpent was not seen as inherently evil, but rather as a symbol of wisdom and enlightenment. This perspective allowed for a different interpretation of the story of the first woman and the serpent. In this fable, the serpent is not trying to lead the woman astray, but rather is helping her to achieve a higher state of being.

Overall, the two stories share many similarities, including the temptation of the first woman by a talking serpent and the pursuit of knowledge and enlightenment. However, the different cultural and religious perspectives of the societies in which they were created led to different portrayals of the serpent, with one being associated with evil and the other with wisdom and knowledge.

Flutes and Trumpets

The story of Amphion and the walls of Thebes comes from Greek mythology and dates back to ancient times, while the story of Joshua and the walls of Jericho comes from the Bible and is believed to have occurred around 1400 BCE. Both stories involve the use of musical instruments to bring about miraculous events, but the context and implications of these stories are quite different.

According to the myth of Amphion, the city of Thebes was in ruins until Amphion, a gifted musician, used his flute to charm the stones into rising from the ground and forming the walls of the city. The story emphasizes the power of music and creativity, and Amphion is revered as a hero for his ability to bring order and civilization to the chaotic world. This story reflects the values of ancient Greek culture, which valued music, art, and intelligence.

On the other hand, the story of Joshua and the walls of Jericho is a biblical account of the Israelites' conquest of the city of Jericho. According to the story, Joshua and his army marched around the walls of Jericho once a day for six days, and on the seventh day, they circled the city seven times while blowing trumpets. As a result, the walls of Jericho miraculously collapsed, allowing the Israelites to take the city. This story reflects the biblical belief in the power of God to intervene in human affairs and the importance of faith in achieving victory.

The story of Amphion using his flute to cause stones to form the walls of Thebes may seem just as incredible and miraculous as the story of Joshua using trumpets to bring down the walls of Jericho. There is no objective measure of the plausibility of miraculous events, and what seems believable or not is often influenced by cultural and religious biases. Therefore, it is important to approach all such stories with a critical eye and evaluate them based on available evidence and logical reasoning, rather than blindly accepting them as true.

The Hermaphrodite

The story of the creation of the first humans in the book of Genesis is a familiar one to many readers, with God forming Adam from the dust of the earth and creating Eve from Adam's rib. However, the story also includes a reference to God creating a hermaphrodite as the first human, before later separating the being into two distinct sexes. This detail has been the subject of much discussion and critique, as it raises questions about the purpose and implications of such a creation.

The miracle of creating a hermaphrodite in Genesis is criticized for not serving the intended purpose and leading to the creation of a purely feminine companion from Adam's rib instead. This raises questions about why God would create a being with both male and female characteristics, only to later separate them into two distinct sexes.

Interestingly, the idea of a hermaphroditic Adam is not unique to the Jewish tradition. It can also be found in Plato's Symposium, where Aristophanes tells a story about how humans used to have four arms, four legs, and two faces. These humans were so powerful that the gods became jealous and split them in two, creating separate male and female beings. Aristophanes suggests that love is the desire to be reunited with one's other half, and that this is the source of all human desire.

The similarities between the Jewish and Platonic traditions suggest that there may be some common origins for these ideas. It is possible that both traditions drew upon earlier myths and legends to create their own stories, or that they independently arrived at similar ideas about the nature of human beings and their relationship to the divine.

Resurrection and Immortality

The Egyptians believed in the concept of an afterlife, where the soul of the deceased would journey to the underworld and be judged by the god Osiris. If the soul was deemed worthy, it would enter the "Field of Reeds," a paradise-like realm for the blessed dead.

The Persians believed in a similar concept of the afterlife, with the soul undergoing a judgment before entering either heaven or hell. In Zoroastrianism, the good souls would go to a place called the "House of Song" or the "House of Good Deeds," while the evil souls would be sent to a place of punishment.

The Greeks had their own beliefs about the afterlife, with the souls of the dead journeying to Hades, the realm of the dead. The souls would be judged by the god Hades and either sent to the Elysian Fields, a paradise-like realm, or to Tartarus, a place of punishment.

It wasn't until after the Babylonian exile that the Jews began to adopt a belief in the resurrection of the dead. This belief was likely influenced by the Zoroastrianism religion of the Persians, who believed in a final judgment and the resurrection of the dead.

Natural Phenomena

The story of the ten plagues of Egypt and the parting of the Red Sea has been subject to much scrutiny and debate among scholars. Some argue that these events were not supernatural miracles, but rather natural phenomena that were exaggerated over time.

For example, the first plague of water turning to blood could have been caused by a toxic red algae bloom, while the fourth plague of flies and gnats could have been the result of a particularly bad mosquito season.

Similarly, the parting of the Red Sea could have been the result of a strong wind that caused the water to recede, allowing the Israelites to cross on dry land. This explanation is supported by the fact that the Hebrew word for "Red Sea" can also mean "reed sea," which would be more shallow and thus more easily parted by a strong wind.

Some scholars argue that these natural explanations do not detract from the religious significance of the story, as the Hebrews would have seen these events as divine intervention regardless of the scientific explanation behind them. However, the fact remains that the story of the ten plagues and the parting of the Red Sea has been attributed to natural phenomena, suggesting that the original story may have been exaggerated over time.

The Garden of Eden

The story of the Garden of Eden, where Adam and Eve were created and subsequently fell from grace, is one of the most well-known stories in the Bible. However, the concept of a garden or paradise is not unique to the Bible, and is found in various ancient myths and fables from different cultures.

In Greek mythology, the Hesperides were nymphs who tended a garden in the far west, where the golden apples of immortality grew. This garden was said to be a gift from the gods, and was guarded by a dragon. The Norse mythology of Valhalla describes a great hall where the bravest warriors go after death. Valhalla is described as a garden or paradise, where the warriors can feast and battle forever.

In Babylonian mythology, there is a Garden of the Gods, which was said to be a place of eternal life and happiness. This garden was said to be the dwelling place of the gods and goddesses, and was located on a sacred mountain. The story of the Garden of Eden in the Bible shares similarities with all these myths, suggesting that the concept of a garden or paradise was a common theme across different cultures.

The idea of a garden or paradise is also associated with the concept of immortality and the afterlife, which is a central theme in many religions. The story of the Garden of Eden in the Bible is an example of how different cultures have used the concept of a garden or paradise to convey their beliefs about the nature of life, death, and the afterlife.

Christianity or Pagan Myths

Jesus' Conception

Romulus and Remus were twin brothers and the legendary founders of Rome. Their mother was a Vestal Virgin named Rhea Silvia, and their father was said to be the god Mars. The story goes that the god Mars visited Rhea Silvia in her sleep and impregnated her with the twins. Similarly, in Christianity, Jesus was born to the virgin Mary and conceived through the Holy Spirit, without any physical involvement from a man.

In Greek mythology, Dionysus was the son of Zeus, the king of the gods, and Semele, a mortal woman. Semele was said to have been impregnated by Zeus while he was disguised as a mortal man. Dionysus was born after Zeus brought him to term by sewing him into his own thigh. Like Jesus, Dionysus was believed to have performed miracles, including turning water into wine, and he was associated with rebirth and resurrection.

In Christianity, Jesus was the son of God and the virgin Mary. He was conceived through the Holy Spirit and born to Mary in a stable in Bethlehem. Jesus is known for his miracles, including turning water into wine and healing the sick, and he is associated with the idea of resurrection and eternal life.

All three stories share similarities in the conception and divine nature of their main figures, as well as their association with miracles and rebirth. These similarities have led some scholars to suggest that the story of Jesus in Christianity was influenced by earlier myths and legends.

Water Into Wine

In the Greek myth of Dionysus, the god is often depicted as a divine figure who performs miracles and transformations, such as turning water into wine. The transformation of water into wine is a symbolic act that represents the divine power of Dionysus, who was associated with wine, fertility, and ecstasy.

Similarly, in the Bible, Jesus performs the miracle of turning water into wine at a wedding in Cana. This miracle is significant as it marks the beginning of Jesus' public ministry and serves as a demonstration of his divine power. The transformation of water into wine also symbolizes the abundance and joy that come with the presence of Jesus in one's life.

In the Hindu legend of the god Indra, he turns water into wine in order to quench the thirst of a group of ascetics who have taken a vow of abstinence. This act of transformation represents Indra's generosity and ability to provide for those in need. It also serves as a reminder of the power of the gods to change the course of nature.

These stories all feature a miraculous transformation of water into wine, symbolizing abundance, joy, and divine power. It is possible that the story of Jesus' miracle at the wedding in Cana was influenced by earlier myths and legends, such as those of Dionysus and Indra.

To Hell and Back

In Greek mythology, Hermes is the god of commerce, invention, and travelers, among other things. He is also known as the messenger of the gods and is often depicted with wings on his sandals and helmet. According to the myth, Hermes was able to travel to and from the underworld or hell at will. He was able to use his powers of persuasion and trickery to convince the god of the underworld, Hades, to release the soul of the recently deceased, which he then brought back to the land of the living.

In Christianity, Jesus is said to have descended into hell after his death and before his resurrection. This idea is based on the belief that Jesus went to the realm of the dead to free the souls of the righteous who had died before his resurrection. Some versions of the story suggest that Jesus also preached to the souls in hell and gave them a chance to repent before his return to heaven.

More Miracles

Asclepius was a Greek god of healing who was known for his ability to bring the dead back to life. He performed many miraculous acts during his lifetime, including healing the sick and curing blindness. Asclepius was said to have been killed by Zeus for his ability to raise the dead but was later resurrected and became a god of medicine.

Hercules was a legendary hero in Greek mythology known for his immense strength and courage. He completed the famous Twelve Labors, which included slaying the Nemean lion and capturing the Cretan bull. Hercules was also said to have performed miracles, such as healing the sick and bringing the dead back to life. According to one legend, he even held up the heavens to save the world from destruction.

Jesus is the central figure of Christianity and is believed to be the son of God. He is said to have performed numerous miracles, such as healing the sick, feeding the multitudes, and even raising the dead. One of the most famous miracles attributed to Jesus is the turning of water into wine at the wedding in Cana.

The similarities between the stories of Asclepius, Hercules, and Jesus are striking. All three figures were known for their miraculous abilities, including healing the sick and raising the dead. They were also associated with resurrection and immortality, with Asclepius and Hercules being brought back to life and Jesus rising from the dead after his crucifixion.

It is likely that the stories of these earlier mythological figures influenced the portrayal of Jesus in the Bible, with his miracles and ability to conquer death drawing on these earlier traditions.

The Infinite God

Theologians have long debated the nature of God and the existence of other beings and existences besides Him. On one hand, they assert that God is infinite, all-powerful, and all-knowing. Yet, on the other hand, they also claim that there are angels, demons, and other supernatural beings that exist alongside God. This seems to be a contradiction in terms, as an infinite God should be the only existence in the universe.

In contrast, the wiser ancient pagans reasoned more consistently about the nature of God. They believed that God made all things out of nothing but Himself, whom they held to be infinite. Therefore, they denied the existence of any other thing besides Him. For them, if anything else exists besides God, then He cannot be infinite, but only co-existent with other things. This concept of God as the only existence in the universe is also found in the philosophy of mystics and pantheists.

The idea of a singular, infinite God also has implications for the understanding of creation and the relationship between God and the universe. In this view, God is not just a creator who made the world and then left it to its own devices, but rather, the universe is a continuous manifestation of God's infinite being. Everything in the universe, from the smallest particle to the largest galaxy, is an expression of God's infinite power and creativity.

While the concept of a singular, infinite God may seem simplistic or limiting to some, it can provide a sense of unity and purpose to believers. It also emphasizes the importance of recognizing the sacredness and interconnectedness of all things in the universe and encourages us to live in harmony with nature and one another.

Chapter Five

There are many individuals today who continue to challenge the role of religion in society and promote critical thinking. Some notable examples include Richard Dawkins, Sam Harris, Christopher Hitchens, and Daniel Dennett, who are often referred to as the "Four Horsemen of New Atheism." They have written extensively on topics such as the harm caused by religion, the compatibility of science and religion, and the need for a secular society. Other notable figures in the skeptical and freethought communities include Susan Jacoby, Lawrence Krauss, and Michael Shermer.

The Four Horsemen of New Atheism are a group of prominent atheists who gained widespread recognition in the early 2000s for their criticism of religion and advocacy for reason and science. The group consists of Richard Dawkins, Sam Harris, Christopher Hitchens, and Daniel Dennett.

Richard Dawkins is an evolutionary biologist and author of the best-selling book "The God Delusion," which argues that belief in God is irrational, and that religious faith is harmful to society. Dawkins is known for his advocacy of science and his criticism of religious belief, which he views as a threat to reason and rationality.

Sam Harris is a neuroscientist and philosopher who has written extensively on the intersection of science, ethics, and religion. His books, including "The End of Faith" and "Letter to a Christian Nation," argue that religion is a source of irrationality, superstition, and intolerance, and that science and reason offer a better path forward.

Christopher Hitchens was a journalist, author, and outspoken atheist who wrote several books, including "God is Not Great: How Religion Poisons Everything." Hitchens was known for his sharp wit and polemical style, and he was a vocal critic of organized religion and its role in society.

Daniel Dennett is a philosopher and cognitive scientist who has written extensively on consciousness, free will, and evolution. His book "Breaking the Spell: Religion as a Natural Phenomenon" argues that religion should be studied scientifically and that its origins can be understood through evolutionary biology and cognitive science.

Together, the Four Horsemen of New Atheism represent a significant force in the contemporary atheism movement, and their work has helped to popularize critical thinking, skepticism, and scientific inquiry as a means of understanding the world and promoting human well-being.

Indigenous

Indigenous peoples around the world have diverse religious beliefs and practices that are often closely tied to their cultural traditions and ways of life. Many indigenous religions emphasize the importance of the land, the natural world, and the relationships between people and their environment.

In many cases, the arrival of colonizers and the spread of Christianity and other world religions has resulted in the suppression and marginalization of indigenous religious beliefs and practices. This has often been accompanied by violence, forced conversion, and the imposition of foreign cultural values on indigenous communities.

Despite this, many indigenous people have worked to preserve and revitalize their traditional religious practices, often in the face of significant obstacles. Some have also sought to integrate aspects of their traditional beliefs with other religions or philosophies in order to create new, hybrid forms of spirituality.

Overall, the experiences of indigenous people with regard to religion highlight the complex ways in which cultural beliefs and practices can be shaped by historical and political forces, and the importance of recognizing and respecting the diversity of religious traditions around the world.

Here are six examples of indigenous people who have worked to preserve and revitalize their traditional religious practices:

Winona LaDuke: LaDuke is an Anishinaabe environmental activist and writer who has fought for Native American land rights and environmental justice. She is also a leader in the Native American spiritual movement and has worked to revitalize traditional Anishinaabe religious practices.

John Trudell: Trudell was a Santee Dakota poet, musician, and political activist who fought for Native American rights and sovereignty. He was also a spiritual leader who incorporated traditional Native American beliefs into his work.

Maria Sabina: Sabina was a Mazatec curandera (traditional healer) from Mexico who is famous for introducing Westerners to the traditional Mazatec practice of using psilocybin mushrooms in spiritual ceremonies. She worked to preserve and revitalize Mazatec religious practices, which had been suppressed by the Spanish colonizers.

Chief Arvol Looking Horse: Looking Horse is a Lakota spiritual leader who holds the title of Keeper of the Sacred White Buffalo Calf Pipe. He has worked to promote traditional Lakota religious practices and has spoken out against the exploitation of Native American spirituality by non-Native people.

Phillip Deere: Deere was a Creek-Seminole activist and spiritual leader who fought for Native American sovereignty and self-determination. He was also a practitioner of the Creek-Seminole religious tradition known as the "Green Corn Ceremony" and worked to promote traditional religious practices among Native American communities.

Taiaiake Alfred: Alfred is a Kanien'kehá:ka (Mohawk) scholar and activist who has written extensively about indigenous nationalism and sovereignty. He is also a practitioner of traditional Mohawk religious practices and has worked to promote the revitalization of these practices among Mohawk communities.

Dr. Micheál Ledwith

Dr. Micheál Ledwith is a former Catholic priest of the Diocese of Ferns in County Wexford from 1967 to 2005.

Ledwith's research interests were focused on theology's fundamental areas that he referred to as the "four great questions": Who are we, where did we come from, what should we do, and where are we going? However, he noticed that none of these questions could provide satisfactory answers about the afterlife, our spiritual development, and what existed before our life on earth. Despite people finding God attractive, he observed that religions claiming to be God's instruments were increasingly dismissed as irrelevant. Dr. Ledwith aimed to discover what went wrong and how the damage could be fixed. He discovered Ramtha's School of Ancient Wisdom, a vast body of teachings that filled the gaps in knowledge and experience of the existing religions. He has been actively studying at the school for years and has lectured at teaching sessions in various countries. His research involved separating time-conditioned modes of thought and views of reality from fundamental beliefs about God and human destiny.

"These are truths that hold the key to the joy, freedom, and power of the new Earth. Religions have constantly suppressed and ruthlessly persecuted those who spoke them."

I recommend you look at his work:

Deep Deceptions Volume 1: The Great Questions in the Hamburger Universe is a book / dvd written by Miceal Ledwith that explores fundamental areas of theology, including questions about human identity, origin, purpose, and destiny. Ledwith critiques existing religions, which he finds have failed to provide convincing information about what happens after death and what individuals should do to aid their spiritual development. He turned to the teachings of Ramtha's School of Ancient Wisdom, which filled gaps in knowledge and experience left by traditional religions. Ledwith's research involves separating time-bound beliefs about reality from fundamental beliefs about God and human destiny.

How Jesus Became a Christ: The Hidden Years: is the second volume of "Deep Deceptions" by Miceal Ledwith. In this book / dvd, Ledwith explores the lesser-known years of Jesus' life and how they contributed to his eventual recognition as the Christ. He delves into topics such as Jesus' travels to the East, his study of the spiritual traditions of other cultures, and his initiation into esoteric knowledge. Ledwith's work challenges traditional interpretations of Jesus and presents a more nuanced and expansive view of his life and teachings.

About the Author

Ethan Knight is a renowned author and intellectual known for his thought-provoking perspectives on religion, philosophy, and the power of free thought. Born into a family deeply rooted in academia and intellectual pursuits, Ethan's early exposure to diverse ideas and critical thinking shaped his intellectual curiosity from a young age.

Throughout his formative years, Ethan displayed a remarkable aptitude for literature, history, and philosophy, eagerly immersing himself in the works of great thinkers and scholars. Fueling his passion for knowledge, he pursued higher education, obtaining a degree in Philosophy and Religious Studies from a prestigious university.

It was during his academic journey that Ethan's deep fascination with the role of religion in society began to take shape. He embarked on an extensive exploration of religious texts, scrutinizing their inconsistencies, contradictions, and the potential suppression of free thought within religious frameworks. This profound inquiry became the impetus for his groundbreaking book, "The Tyranny of Belief: How Religion Suppresses Free Thought."

Published to critical acclaim, "The Tyranny of Belief" garnered widespread attention for its incisive analysis and thought-provoking arguments. In this seminal work, Ethan challenges the notion that blind belief in religious dogma is beneficial to society. Instead, he shines a light on the potential dangers of unquestioning faith, the suppression of critical thinking, and the manipulation of religious power structures.

Ethan Knight's scholarship and eloquence have made him a sought-after speaker at conferences and seminars worldwide. His thought-provoking lectures and insightful discussions have captivated audiences, igniting conversations and encouraging individuals to reevaluate their perspectives on religion, spirituality, and personal freedom.

Beyond his written works and public appearances, Ethan remains deeply committed to promoting open dialogue and intellectual freedom. He continues to engage in scholarly research, contributing to academic journals and participating in interdisciplinary collaborations that explore the intersection of religion, philosophy, and human rights.

As a prolific writer and influential thinker, Ethan Knight has left an indelible mark on the intellectual landscape, challenging conventional wisdom and inspiring readers to embrace critical thinking and pursue truth. His relentless pursuit of knowledge and unwavering dedication to the pursuit of intellectual freedom make him a leading voice in the ongoing discourse on the relationship between religion and free thought.